How to Draw
ANYTHING

How to Draw
ANYTHING
A complete guide

Angela Gair

p

This is a Parragon Publishing Book
This edition published in 2004

Parragon Publishing
Queen Street House
4 Queen Street
Bath BA1 1HE, UK

ISBN: 1-40543-031-1

Printed in China

Acknowledgements
Art Director: Ron Samuels
Editor: Jo-Anne Cox
Design: Zoë Mellors
Photography: Jeff Lee

All the illustrations are by Stephen Dew except for the projects on pages 53-55
and 118-121 which are by John Palmer, and the flowers on page 145
which are by Zoë Mellors.

CONTENTS

INTRODUCTION

Anyone who can hold a pencil can learn to draw. Contrary to popular belief, talented artists are made and not born, and they have to work hard in order to achieve their goals. After all, who would expect a musician to play a Mozart concerto without first learning to read music and spending many hours practicing piano scales? Who would expect an athlete to win the Olympics without putting in grueling hours of training? It is no different for the artist. To develop your drawing skills and achieve proficiency in your art, you need to draw and sketch regularly.

Of course, it's not all plain sailing. Making that first mark on a pristine sheet of white paper is a little like being the first person to trample across a patch of crisp, freshly fallen snow—it seems such a shame to spoil it! Add to this the fear of failure, of not being able to reach the high standards we have set for ourselves, and it is easy to see why people give up drawing before they have begun. If you are

unsure about your ability to draw, the best way to increase your confidence is to do small sketches on a regular basis, rather than attempting a finished drawing only occasionally. Carry a small sketchbook with you wherever you go so that, whenever you see something that inspires you, you can just open it up and get to work, even if you only have a few minutes to spare. Try to develop your observational skills, learning how to look at a flower, or a cloud,

or an apple, just as a child would, with a fresh eye and a sense of wonder. Sketch anything and everything—people and places, animals and birds, landscapes and cityscapes. Use any medium you feel comfortable with—a pencil, a felt-tip marker, a ballpoint pen. The point is to train your hand to respond to what you see, immediately and instinctively, without worrying about making a "perfect" drawing. Accept the fact that, to begin with, many of your drawings will be failures, and just enjoy the sheer pleasure of the drawing process. Keep all your sketches, including the disasters, and you will be able to see how much progress you have made. You will be surprised at how quickly your drawing skills improve if you manage to work regularly. I always say, "A drawing a day makes the fear go away!"

Essentially, the secret of learning to draw is learning to enjoy drawing purely for its own sake. Drawing is an immensely pleasurable activity. A good drawing session can be compared to yoga or meditation; when you are drawing something that really engages your interest you are completely absorbed, all your worries and woes are forgotten and you emerge refreshed and relaxed.

You will find in this book plenty of information about the fundamentals of drawing; perspective,

proportion, color, line and tone, and how to use particular techniques and materials to express your ideas. Projects in every chapter guide you step-by-step to achieving a complete drawing. Essentially, though, it is not a "how-to-do it" book; it is more a "how-to-see-it" book, designed to encourage you to observe and analyze particular visual aspects of your subject—forms, tones, textures, proportions—and then find a way to express, through mark-making, your emotional response to that subject. For it is my belief that all the skills and techniques in the world are not much use if you don't have something interesting to say about the world around you—and that can only come about by looking at the world with an inquiring eye.

DRAWING MATERIALS

All you really need to make a sketch or drawing is a pencil and a piece of paper. However, one of the delights of drawing lies in the large and diverse range of materials that you can choose from. In addition, several traditional media such as charcoal and pastels are now produced in a convenient pencil form that makes them much easier to use when traveling, when you want a selection of lightweight materials that will also give you as much scope as possible for trying different approaches.

Keep an open mind about what to use for different types of drawings, and experiment with a variety of materials to see what they feel like and what effects they can produce. Avoid buying big sets of colored pencils, pastels, or paints, because they are expensive and often contain colors you don't need. Buy pastels and pencils in a few colors, or select a few individual tubes or pans of paint.

Keep your drawing materials light so that they will easily fit into a bag and not be a burden when you are out and about looking for subjects. For working on loose sheets of paper rather than sketchbooks and pads, you will need a drawing board. A sketching easel—available in either wood or metal—is an asset.

PENCILS

The simple pencil is a supremely versatile drawing instrument. It can be used to create lines and marks that vary greatly in character; it can be used for tonal drawings; it can be easily erased and reworked; and it can be combined with other media, such as pen and ink.

Graphite pencils come in several grades, from very hard to very soft: H to 6H, designating hard to very hard; HB to 9B, soft to very soft. **Charcoal pencils** are available in a small range of grays from light to dark; they smudge quite easily. **Conté pencils**, which are available in earth reds and browns, black, and white, have a more waxy, and sometimes a rougher feel than graphite and charcoal pencils. Some are not easy to smudge effectively, but they produce a soft, flowing line.

Graphite pencils can be used with any type of paper surface, depending on whether you want a smooth, even, continuous line or a broken, rough, or darker-toned effect. Charcoal pencils are best used on medium and rough papers.

To start drawing, you will need HB, 2B, 4B, and 6B graphite pencils, a charcoal pencil, and some conté pencils. The best way to sharpen pencils is with a craft knife, which enables you to bring the pencil to a sharp point while wasting very little lead.

CHARCOAL

Charcoal is an extremely expressive drawing tool. The slightest touch of charcoal to paper will produce a subtle mark, and the range of tones you can achieve with it is endless. There are two types of charcoal: vine and compressed. **Vine charcoal sticks** come in various thicknesses from thin to thick. The thinner sticks, in particular, break easily if used vigorously. You can use charcoal on its end to create lines, or on its side to block in large areas of tone, and you can smudge it easily for a soft effect. The speed with which you can use charcoal, whether for line or tone, makes it particularly well-suited for large-scale work. **Compressed charcoal** is much more waxy than vine charcoal, and produces darker marks that are more difficult to manipulate on the paper.

When choosing paper for charcoal work, go for medium or rough surfaces, rather than smooth surfaces, because the pits in the paper pick up and hold more charcoal, making it much easier to produce rich, dark tones. A textured paper also breaks up denser areas of tone. Handle charcoal carefully, and once you have completed a drawing, always fix it immediately to prevent the charcoal from accidentally smudging or moving (see page 11).

CONTE CRAYONS

These come in the form of square or round sticks. They are more chalky than conté pencils, but are not as soft as vine charcoal. They are available in black, white, and a range of warm and cool grays, and in a variety of red and brown earth colors such as terracotta, Venetian red, sanguine, and sepia. Conté crayons work particularly well on colored papers, especially mid-toned grays and warm earth colors, with the paper being allowed to show through as one of the tones or colors in the drawing.

PEN & INK

An ever-increasing range of **pens** is available, including traditional dip and mapping pens with steel nibs, refillable fountain pens with drawing nibs (an italic nib can also be used for drawing), various rollerball and felt-tip types, and technical drawing pens. Steel drawing nibs broaden under pressure, making it easy to produce variations in a line. When you're starting out, a pen with interchangeable nibs is your best option, plus one or two rollerball or technical pens for convenience when you are doing quick sketches.

Inks come in black and a range of other colors. There are two types: waterproof and water-soluble. If you are using a pen line in conjunction with washes, make sure you use a waterproof ink, or the water from the paint will blur the ink lines. You can vary the tonal quality of an ink line by diluting the ink to varying degrees, which gives dip and fountain pens another expressive advantage over other types. The character of the line can also be varied by working on dampened rather than dry paper.

When working in pen and ink, choose smooth watercolor paper, which has a pre-sized surface. If you use ink on an unsized surface it may be absorbed by the paper, producing a fuzzy line.

Felt-tip markers come in thin and broad-tipped varieties and a large range of colors. Look for water-based rather than alcohol-based pens, because the latter may "bleed" into the paper and go right through, which would be annoying if you are using a sketchbook.

COLORED PENCILS

There are various types of colored pencils on the market, all offering different qualities and possibilities. You will find that colored pencils vary greatly in softness, depending on the manufacturer. Some produce soft colors, even in the stronger, darker tones, while others produce far more intense colors. All good-quality pencils ought to be firm in texture and you should be able to bring them to a sharp point. You can use colored pencils to draw with line, or to shade in areas of color with closely hatched lines. Of course you can't mix colors the way you can with paints, but you will discover a variety of optical and broken-color mixing techniques that produce either subtle or vibrant effects.

Water-soluble pencils will enable you to combine drawing and painting within the same medium, and you can use them in a number of ways. The most common and useful method is to draw with them onto your paper, before dissolving the color with a brush loaded with water to produce

flat washes or to blend two or more colors. Lines worked over damp paper will spread slightly and have a soft, furred quality.

PASTELS & CHALKS

Pastels and chalks allow for a spontaneous and expressive approach to sketching. **Soft pastels** have a wonderful chalky, smudgy quality and are available in a wide range of colors and tints. They come in round and square forms, and can be bought in boxed sets or singly. **Pastel sticks** are more versatile than **pastel pencils**, but not so convenient when you are traveling or sketching on location.

Drawing chalks are harder in texture than pastels, and less easy to move around and smudge once they are applied to the paper.

Oil pastels have a soft, slightly greasy quality. They come in a smaller range of colors than soft pastels, and are very difficult to manipulate on the paper. However, they are soluble in turpentine and can be applied and then rubbed and blended with a cloth or cotton swap dipped in turpentine to produce a smooth, transparent layer of color. Another way to use them is to apply layers of color on the paper and then scrape off or draw into the top layers to reveal the color underneath.

Pastels can be used with any paper that has a slight tooth. Textured pastel papers are available in a wide range of colors, and medium and rough watercolor papers can also be used. Artists'-quality sandpaper for use with soft pastels is available from art supply stores, and is an excellent surface if you want to build up several layers of color.

Soft pastels and chalks are easily rubbed or

smudged accidentally, so to avoid mistakes, fix them when you have finished (see below right). Drawings should also be stored carefully. Tape a sheet of tracing paper in place over them to stop anything from rubbing against the surface.

PAINTS & BRUSHES

Paints provide exciting and flexible media for sketching, whether you use them on their own or combined with other media. Watercolor, gouache, and acrylics are convenient to use and light to carry, and it isn't necessary to work with a large range of colors. **Watercolors** are available in small sketching sets and individual tubes or pans of paint.

Brushes for drawing are generally the soft, springy type used for watercolor painting. These are available in either sable, sable/synthetic mixtures, or synthetic fibers. Sable brushes are expensive, but they have a wonderful springiness in the bristles and last a long time. Chinese brushes, usually made of goat's hair and with bamboo handles, also provide excellent drawing tools. Brushes can be used with paints or drawing inks, and they can be used either loaded with paint, or fairly dry for a dragged effect.

PAPERS & ACCESSORIES

The overall impression that a drawing makes results from the interaction between the medium used and the paper texture, so the choice of paper for a drawing is important. Some papers are more suitable for use with particular media than others, so make sure you choose the most suitable option.

There are three main categories of paper surface for drawing and watercolor papers: HP (hot pressed) or smooth, NOT (cold-pressed) or medium rough; and rough. Papers also vary in weight, which is expressed in pounds, usually indicated by the symbol #. A lightweight drawing or watercolor paper is about 70-pound (70#), and a heavy watercolor paper is 140-pound (140#).

Other essential accessories are a drawing board, masking tape or clips, fixative, erasers, a craft knife for sharpening pencils, and palettes for mixing washes and colors.

FIXING A DRAWING

Drawings done with graphite pencils, pastels, charcoal, or chalks need to be fixed to prevent them from being damaged during framing or storage. Fixative is available in aerosols, or in bottles for use with a diffuser spray. The diffuser has two sections set at a right angle, and is used by dipping the end of one section in the fixative and blowing through the mouthpiece on the other section.

It is important not to soak the drawing with fixative, as this will dull the medium used. To avoid this effect, don't point the fixative directly at the drawing. Instead, lay the paper flat and spray onto it horizontally, letting the fixative fall onto the drawing in a fine shower. Move the can from side to side across the full width of the paper, working from top to bottom, to give the drawing a light but even coverage. It is better to apply two light coats, letting the first dry, rather than one heavy coat, which is more likely to affect the quality of the artwork. Spray onto newspaper first to practice the technique.

11

CHAPTER 1

LANDSCAPES

To gaze in awe at great mountains, to watch sunshine and cloud pass over a green patchwork of field and forest, to stand by a river, lake or seashore watching the constant movement of water and light refreshes our spirits. Finding pleasure and delight in the beauty and grandeur of our natural surroundings seems to be one of the most basic human emotions—and so must be the urge to capture it in some way and record it forever.

One advantage for the artist that the landscape has over other themes is that it is present all the time, and it is all around us. Unlike animals and human beings, it stays still and is infinitely patient. Not that there aren't any changes—climate and weather take care of that! But the effects of wind and rain, sunshine and cloud are the very things that make any landscape scene so fascinating to draw.

The one disadvantage is that there is so much area to cover. Wherever you turn your eyes, there are so many features, shapes and surfaces, textures and tones, and colors. It often seems impossible to set down on paper one fraction of all that detail.

You must decide on the composition of your picture—viewpoint, how much of the subject to include, and overall shape. Then you will have to set down on paper the different features of the scene, its forms and structures, its tonal pattern, and relate all these to each other using the rules of perspective. You will soon discover the importance and pleasure of keeping a sketchbook to record information about places, objects and effects for later use.

Drawing is all about the way we perceive the world around us, which may be why artists turn so readily to landscapes and natural objects as a source of inspiration. You may, like Monet, want to explore light, or, like Cézanne, investigate structure. You may wish to translate the moods of nature into paint, like Constable, or to penetrate the essential force of nature, like Turner. But whatever you are searching for in art, you will find it in a landscape.

COMPOSING A SCENE

Composition is the process of arranging the different elements of the subject on paper so that the eye is directed to the main area of interest. The most important decisions you have to make about composition when sketching are: the angle of view, how much of the subject to include and the overall shape of the subject.

Before selecting the final composition, you should look at the subject from several different angles. You can either work on the same level as the subject, get above it and look down, or get down low and look up. A change of viewpoint can often make a mundane subject suddenly look exciting.

The horizon exists on a level with your eye, so from a high viewpoint you get a high horizon and from a low viewpoint a low horizon. If you cannot see the horizon, you can judge where it would be by establishing your eye level: hold up a pencil in a horizontal position in front of your eyes and note where it intersects with the subject. This is your eye level. One of the first decisions you need to make is where you are going to position the eye level on the paper—or what alternative viewpoint you are going to take.

Often several options face you when framing and composing a picture. It can be difficult to decide how much to include and whether to make the composition vertical or horizontal. Do thumbnail sketches before starting the actual drawing. You can either use your hands to frame the subject while you assess it or use a viewfinder—a rectangle cut out of the center of a piece of cardboard (see page 17).

The distance between you and different elements in your subject area affects how you see each of them. The farther away an object is, the smaller it will look in relation to things near you, regardless of their relative sizes if placed next to each other.

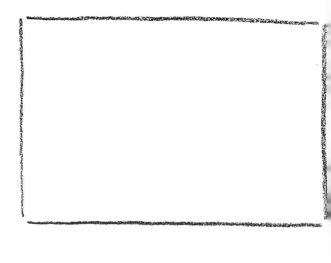

▶ THUMBNAIL
SKETCHES

In framing and composing a picture, preliminary thumbnail sketches help establish your viewpoint, how much of the subject you want to include, and what overall shape it should have.

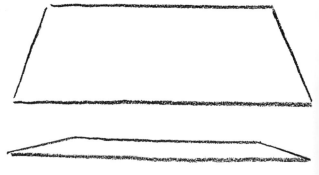

▲ RECTANGLES

The opposite sides of a rectangle are parallel when it is viewed head-on. The greater the angle at which the rectangle is seen, the more sharply the sides converge, and the narrower it becomes from front to back.

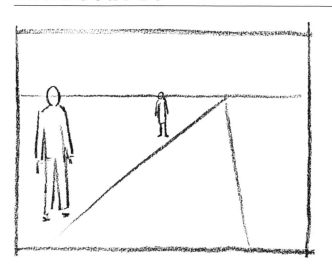

▼▲ SCALE & SHAPE

Figures and objects that are closer to you will appear larger than those that are positioned farther away.

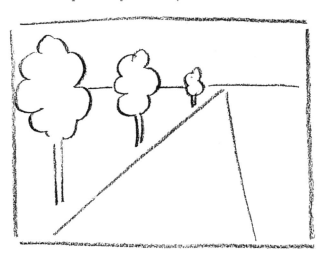

▲ VERTICAL RECTANGLES

The same effect is seen in rectangles with the longer sides vertical (top and center). Even seen from a corner (bottom), the rectangle has slightly converging sides.

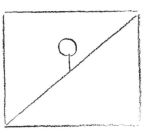

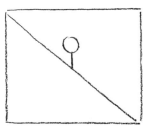

◄ DIAGONALS

Most people read a picture from left to right. The picture on the left thus appears to go uphill, while the picture below left appears to slope downhill.

As a simple experiment, try holding your hands out in front of you, with one hand close to your face and the other as far away as possible. Now overlap them slightly and look at them with one eye closed. Notice where the tips of the fingers and the base of your further hand intercept the nearer hand, and how much smaller the further hand now appears. When including objects that exist on different planes in your drawing, the size of each must be logical in relation to their position in space. The fact that the closer something is to you, the larger it appears—known as foreshortening—affects everything you draw.

A more formal approach to getting the different elements in a scene in the right scale is through the use of linear perspective. This system of reproducing three-dimensional objects on a flat surface so that they recede in space and sit squarely on the ground is based on the fact that all parallel lines leading away from the viewer appear to converge at the horizon. The point at which parallel lines actually converge is known as the vanishing point and represents infinity. This phenomenon has suggested the solution to the problem of how to represent objects at different distances away from an observer in the correct scale.

Perspective affects two- and three-dimensional shapes and forms. A rectangle viewed head-on has both horizontal sides and vertical sides parallel (see pages 14-15). When the rectangle is tilted forward or backward, the horizontal sides remain parallel, but the vertical sides, which extend away from the viewer, start to converge. The more the rectangle is tilted, the more sharply the sides converge.

▲ ▶ HORIZON LEVEL

Where you place the horizon in a drawing has a strong effect on its atmosphere. If the horizon is placed high in the picture (above), it appears to be near and creates a closed-in, claustrophobic impression. A low horizon (right), with little land left below it, seems to be far away, thus emphasizing the sky and evoking a strong feeling of space and freedom.

MAKING & USING A VIEWFINDER

◀ ALTERNATIVES

When composing a landscape, take time to look at the various options available to you in a scene. Here, you can include the whole view, or reduce your area of interest gradually until you end up with a close-up of the buildings. Using a viewfinder is a quick way to explore the alternatives. However you decide to frame such a view, make sure that the focus of interest is placed off-center.

▶ MAKING A VIEWFINDER

The simplest method of making a viewfinder is to cut out two L-shaped pieces of black cardboard, which are large enough to be placed together as shown (right) and moved around until you find the best viewpoint.

MAKING SKETCHES

Sketchbooks are ideal for recording lots of information about a particular place which can be used at a later date in the development of full-scale paintings and drawings.

Having selected a particular landscape scene, work quickly and complete what you want to do in one session. You will probably need to do this anyway because elements in the subject, such as people, the sky and the effects of light and shadow, will be constantly moving and changing. Record as much information as you can about different aspects of the scene. Begin with quick drawings from various viewpoints to help you assess which aspects of the subject have strong compositional elements. These will also help you to understand the forms and

structures within the subject and decide how much to include if you go on to make a more finished drawing. Next, make a charcoal or pencil drawing to record the subject's tonal pattern.

The color can be recorded either in separate color sketches made with color pencils or pastels, or with color washes over a line drawing, or by color swatches or written notes. Note down the date, time of year, time of day, weather conditions and the direction of the light as a reminder for later use. Make small drawings of specific details,

patterns and textures within the subject. These, together with additional material such as postcards, photographs, and found objects like leaves or grasses, which you can stick into the sketchbook, add interest and may also be useful later. It is surprising how one often doesn't have enough detailed information for larger works.

VARYING YOUR MEDIA

Although using just one medium on a sketchbook page may be the easiest option, you can get new ideas from mixing media and subjects. Fine pen and ink lines capture small details and subjects, while graphite and colored pencils block in forms quickly and effectively.

FIELDS & HILLS

When walking in the countryside it is always thrilling to gaze at the fields and hills stretched out as far as the eye can see. For the artist, creating this illusion on a small piece of paper can be equally thrilling—and it's easy once you know how.

One way of creating a sense of depth in a landscape drawing is through linear perspective making objects appear to diminish in size as they recede toward the horizon. Vertical objects such as trees, hills and fences will obviously appear smaller as they recede into the distance, and horizontal areas such as fields appear smaller and narrower. If you are not sure of the height of, say, a tree in the distance compared with a tree in the foreground, you can check using the "measure-and-compare" method. Use the foreground tree as your "key measure", comparing all parts of the subject to that. Hold your pencil at arm's length, elbow locked, in front of the tree. Keeping one eye closed, line up the tip of

the pencil with the top of the tree and mark the position of the base of the trunk with your thumbnail. This is your key measure. Now, keeping your thumbnail in position and your arm outstretched, move the pencil to the distant tree and compare its height with the length of your key measure. You can compare the length of your key measure with

▶ MEASURING

Use your thumb to measure off the subject height on a pencil.

▼ AERIAL PERSPECTIVE

A sense of depth and distance is created through the progressive lightening of tones in a scene as it recedes towards the horizon.

▶ CONVERGING LINES

Lines traveling inward from the foreground to the background carry the eye toward the horizon and give a dynamic sense of depth to this simple sketch.

◀ VARIED MARKS

Use rapid, scribbled marks that follow the undulations in the landscape and suggest the texture of fields and grass without overstatement.

other parts of the landscape, too, for measuring widths as well as heights.

Perhaps the most effective way to create a sense of space and distance in your drawings is through aerial perspective. This describes the way in which atmosphere and haze cause landscape features to become progressively paler and less distinct as they recede towards the horizon. In addition, colors become cooler and "bluer". You can make use of this effect to give a strong sense of space in your drawings. Try to divide your composition into three distinct planes going back in space—foreground, middle ground, and background. Reserve your darkest tones and strongest detail for the foreground, and make the middle ground and background progressively paler and less defined.

Colors in the distance appear cooler, bluer and more muted than those in the foreground. This will create a sense of spatial recession in a drawing. Here, for example, warm, strong, bright colors are used in the foreground, and progressively cooler, paler blue-grays are used in the distance.

In using color to capture a landscape scene, first decide whether the colors you actually see are light or dark, warm or cool. Pay attention to areas of highlight and shadow, and look for colors reflected from other objects.

Color can be used to model form and create a sense of three-dimensional space. Warm colors placed near cool ones tend to advance in a drawing, whereas cool colors tend to recede when seen against warm ones, which creates a sense of space receding into the distance. Space can be conveyed through the contrast between bright colors, which tend to advance, and duller colors, which recede.

Color can also be used in an expressive and atmospheric way. To convey a particular sense of place, use a limited palette of four colors: a version of each of the primaries, plus an earth color or a green such as viridian, plus white. For a warm scene, choose mainly red, yellow, and orange colors, and for a cool scene, use blue, violet, or green colors, but always include a contrasting note to set off the predominant mood. A limited palette will also allow you to work in more neutral, subtle grays, while allowing for touches of bright color here and there.

WARM

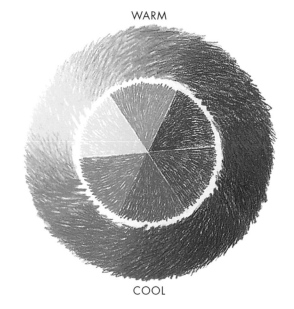

COOL

▲ COLOR TEMPERATURE

The color wheel is made up of the six colors of the spectrum arranged in a circle. The color wheel can be divided in half, one side containing the warm colors—red, yellow and orange—and the other half containing the cool colors—blue, violet and green. Warm colors appear to advance (come towards you) and cool colors recede (move back). You can capitalize on this to describe three-dimensional space, as in the drawing above.

PROJECT: COUNTRY SCENE

To capturing a country scene, you don't have to make a precise drawing of it. You can reduce it to its component parts of form, patterns, and textures and develop them until they actually describe the subject through the medium. Instead of drawing outlines or creating blocks of tone, develop different types of pencil marks and set them against each other to convey the variety of foliage, crops, hills and sky that make up the scene before you.

A country scene is well suited to this approach because of the range of different forms, textures, and patterns usually found within it. Choose a view with a mixture of features that create distinct lines and patterns to give you plenty of material to work with.

There are no rules to limit or control the marks you make: the only criterion is their appropriateness to your subject. Work freely, letting the pencil follow patterns and directions, planes and surfaces. To reduce features to their essential characteristics, decide on their overriding quality and convey just that—spiky bushes, grasses bending in the breeze, or lines of crops. Apply the rules of linear and aerial perspective (see pages 16 and 21) and reduce the weight and size of the marks in the distance in relation to those in the foreground to suggest recession and keep objects in the foreground and distance in the correct scale.

Start by working with a range of pencils from 2B to very soft on a smooth or medium paper. Once your confidence has grown, you could try pen and ink, or incorporate color by using colored pencils or felt-tip markers.

SIMPLIFICATION

When you are out in the country with your sketchbook, try sketching individual features, such as spiky bushes and grasses bending in the wind. Look for ways of reducing these to their essential characteristics, and experiment with a range of different methods of conveying texture, pattern, and a sense of solidity.

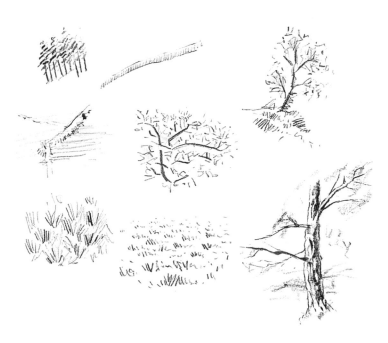

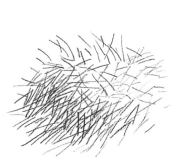

◀ LIGHT & DARK

Strong light and dark contrasts are used here to describe the huts, provide variation in texture and focus the attention of the viewer on that particular area.

▶ CROPS & FOLIAGE

Instead of drawing outlines or creating solid blocks of tone, different types of pencil marks and scribbles are set against each other to delineate complex elements such as foliage and crops, and to indicate their texture.

◀ INDICATING SCALE

To suggest recession and keep objects in the foreground and distance in the correct scale, the weight and size of the pencil marks is reduced and simplified as the scene recedes into the far distance.

◀ WEIGHT & DENSITY

*Three-dimensional modeling
is suggested by varying the
weight and density from one
side of the bush to the other.*

**▲ CONTRASTING &
VARYING MARKS**

*The different elements in the
composition are seen as forms
and shapes that are plotted by
setting one type of mark
against another. The character
of the marks embodies the
surface and textural qualities
of each.*

SKIES & WEATHER

The appearance of the landscape is affected by the season of the year, the time of day and the weather, and these play an important part in establishing mood and atmosphere in your landscape drawings. Following the example of the French Impressionist Claude Monet, make a series of drawings of the same scene at different times of the day or under different weather conditions. Notice the different moods created as the amount, direction and color of the light changes. For example, a landscape at noon might look flat and uninteresting because the light is even and there is very little contrast between light and shadow. But a few hours later, at sunset, long shadows travel across the contours of the land and the luminous tones of the evening sky contrast with the cool, dark tones below.

◄▲ TONAL KEY

A "high-key" drawing made with mid-to-light tones has a light feel (left). A "low-key" drawing made with darker tones has a more brooding atmosphere (above).

▼► EXPRESSIVE COLOR

Think about how you can use color to express atmosphere. The first sketch (below) faithfully records the colors of the landscape. In the second sketch (right) warm yellows and browns have been used everywhere; they do not relate to the actual colors of the subject, but they convey an impression of intense warmth and light.

▲ FOG & MIST

Fog and mist act like a veil over the landscape, turning hills and trees into eerie shapes. Soft media such as charcoal, chalks and pastels can be smudged and blended and are excellent for capturing the effects of fog and mist.

▶ SNOW

A snow-covered landscape on a dark winter day creates strong, almost abstract patterns of light and dark, perfect for a pen-and-ink drawing that captures a feeling of bleakness and silent isolation.

SKIES & CLOUDS

Before you actually start to draw the sky and clouds, watch the changing patterns above you, then make rapid, on-the-spot sketches like these. Clouds can change shape very quickly, and a broad medium, such as pen and wash, charcoal, or pastel, is ideal for capturing them.

The use of light and shade—tonal contrast—is the most effective means of creating a particular mood or atmosphere, or conveying a particular season or weather effect. Sharp contrasts of light and dark will, for example, help to evoke the brilliant light of a summer day; the use of pale, delicate tones evokes the mood of spring; and the drama of a storm can be expressed through the use of predominantly dark tones.

Viewpoint and composition are also important elements in creating mood. The brooding atmosphere of an approaching storm is made more dramatic by placing the horizon line as low down as possible, to place emphasis on the sky. On a sunny day you could try positioning yourself so that much of the subject is in shadow, except for one telling, sunlit spot. This will create a more exciting and unusual picture than if the subject were evenly lit.

Choose a drawing medium that is appropriate for the subject and the mood you wish to convey. A beach scene in midsummer is full of color and high-key tones, ideal for a pastel drawing. A snow-bound farm under a dark winter sky provides the perfect subject for a calligraphic pen-and-ink drawing. Experiment with different drawing materials frequently to find which ones work best.

PROJECT: WINTER NIGHT

Pastels are an ideal medium for creating atmosphere through color and expressive marks. You don't need to reproduce the colors you see. Instead, start by analyzing the mood of the scene, and select a small number of colors that reflect it. Choose a maximum of five or six colors and a medium-toned paper that doesn't contrast strongly with the colors or tones used.

The scene chosen for this project is a cold winter night, with frost on the ground and moonlight catching the tops of the clouds. The cold atmosphere is created with Prussian blue, with its coldness being emphasized by the mid-toned blue paper. A very light tint of Prussian blue is used to describe the frosty ground. Black provides the contrast in tone that creates the strong light catching the tops of the clouds.

The power of color to create or negate space means that you can use it to evoke big spaces and distant horizons, or a heavy, brooding, close atmosphere. Here, the use of the same strong tones and colors in the sky and the land at the horizon, as well as in the nearer parts of the drawing, flattens the image and increases the brooding character of the sky. The horizon is low, so the composition comprises mainly sky, which heightens the drama of the scene.

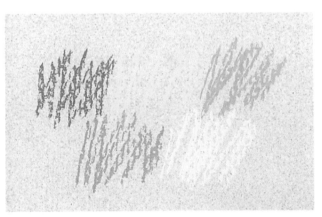

▲ ▶ ATMOSPHERIC PALETTES

The palette for this project runs from a light cobalt blue to a deep Prussian blue, with black for the darkest tone. The two palettes above create different moods: on the gray-green paper, the colors of an early summer morning; on the buff paper, hot, prairie colors. Choose colors that reflect the mood you want to create.

▲ ROUGH BLENDING

Pastel colors can be partially blended together on the paper to create not only interesting color effects but also a lively surface texture and a sense of movement.

▼ REFLECTED LIGHT

Dark blue pastel is laid over light blue, and both are then dragged with a finger to effectively convey reflected light in the sky.

◀ CLOUDS

The clouds are built up with strong contrasts between the lightest and darkest tones, which places the main focus of interest there. The dark, brooding colors give the clouds solidity and volume.

▼ AERIAL RECESSION

A few touches of blue-violet, which appear warm against the cold, pure blues, are used to pull some of the sky forwards in the picture plane. This contrast creates an impression of depth and great distance.

▲ COLORS FOR MOOD

The colors used are not the actual colors in the scene, but they convey a sense of intense cold and a dark, heavy sky animated by intense patches of light. All the colors have been used throughout the drawing. No color distinction has been made between sky and land, although the tonal balance varies, the land being light with touches of dark and the sky mainly dark tones with touches of light.

▶ MID-TONES

The mid-toned gray paper shows through both light and dark areas, providing a lighter tone against the dark colors, and a darker tone against the light areas.

WATERSCAPES

Water is one of the most fascinating and attractive subjects to draw. Whether the subject is a peaceful lake or river with its mirror-like reflections, or a fast-running stream tumbling over rocks, it provides a never-ending source of inspiration. In addition, there are features such as boats, bridges, trees and figures that can be introduced into your waterscapes to add interest and liven the composition.

Water does present the artist with particular problems because of its qualities of reflectivity and transparency. However, there are a few pointers that will help you create a convincing image.

One of the most obvious features are the reflections on the water's surface. They fall immediately beneath the objects casting them, and appear to go straight down into the water—unlike shadows, they don't appear to extend toward the

viewer. Another point to notice is that the closer the reflection is to the object being reflected, the sharper it is, and as it extends away from the object it becomes progressively more blurred and soft-edged.

If the surface of the water is broken up by a breeze or current, the mirror-like reflection becomes broken up, elongated and distorted. Broken reflections usually appear longer than reflections in calm water. The laws of perspective apply to broken reflections. The closer the ripples are to you, the larger and more spread out they appear. Farther away, they appear smaller and closer together.

Tones and colors in reflections are slightly cooler and more muted than those in the objects causing them. The reflections of light objects are always slightly darker than the objects themselves, while dark objects appear slightly lighter when reflected. Careful assessment of the tonal values of reflections against those in the objects creating them is always

▶ RAPID WATER

To draw the rushing, white water of rapids and waterfalls, use light, scribbled strokes on rough-textured paper to suggest detail and movement without "freezing" the action.

▲ CHOOSING A VIEWPOINT

Look for interesting viewpoints when composing waterscapes. Here, the old stone bridge and its mirror reflection in the water create a charming image and form a link between the various elements of the composition.

▶ USING CHARCOAL

A soft medium, such as charcoal, pastel or chalk, is excellent for portraying water. Here, the artist indicated the trees on the riverbank and their reflections in the water by using a short piece of charcoal on its side. He then rubbed the charcoal marks to soften and blend them.

◀ QUICK SKETCHES

Take every opportunity to make quick notes and sketches when you are out. Even a few rapidly drawn lines can prove useful when you sit down to create the final drawing.

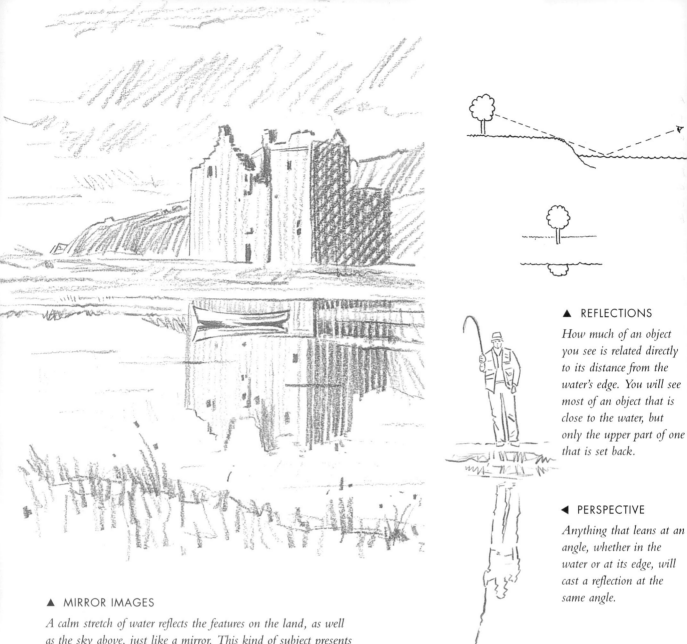

How much of an object you see is related directly to its distance from the water's edge. You will see most of an object that is close to the water, but only the upper part of one that is set back.

◄ PERSPECTIVE

Anything that leans at an angle, whether in the water or at its edge, will cast a reflection at the same angle.

▲ MIRROR IMAGES

A calm stretch of water reflects the features on the land, as well as the sky above, just like a mirror. This kind of subject presents a balanced and satisfying image.

needed; you will find it easier to see the subtle differences if you look at the subject through half-closed eyes.

When an object is set back from the water's edge, only the upper part is reflected. The amount you can see is directly related to the object's distance from the water's edge; again, this will require careful observation. An object that is upright in water—such as a mooring pole—produces a reflection of the same length. However, an object leaning towards you always creates a reflection that is longer than itself, and an object leaning away from

you creates a reflection that is slightly shorter than itself. These principles may apply to the side of a boat, a house, or a tree—any reflected object.

Reflections shouldn't be confused with shadows. Reflections are a mirror image of the surroundings, whereas shadows are cast by objects that block the light. Your best approach is to sit by the waterside and observe very closely the patterns on the water, then make lots of small sketches and studies. Try to see the water surface as a pattern or mosaic of tones and colors and then just concentrate on recording this pattern.

ABSTRACT PATTERNS

When the water's surface is disturbed by ripples or swells, or by raindrops, fascinating patterns can be seen. These are worth studying for their own sake or as part of the bigger picture.

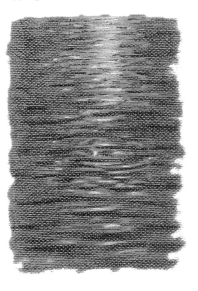

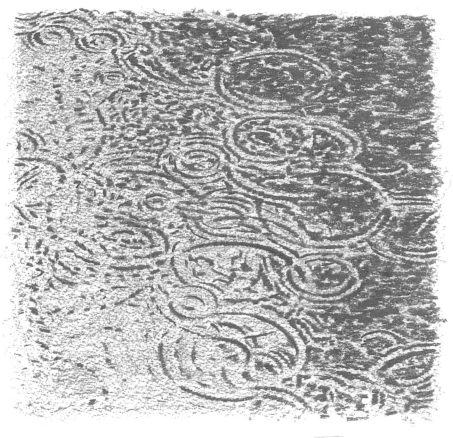

The reflections and highlights on the water's surface sometimes look fairly complicated, but rather than trying to copy every detail, it is better to simplify the patterns. Look at the water through half-closed eyes and pick out the most obvious ripples and reflections. Concentrate on these bigger shapes and cut out any unnecessary detail—otherwise your subject will begin to resemble a patterned carpet rather than the smooth glassy surface of water!

By carefully arranging the lights and darks (the tonal values) in a drawing, it is possible to capture a particular mood or convey the effect of light at a certain time of day. Let light tones predominate if you want to create a bright, high-key mood. Let dark tones predominate if you want to create a low-key, atmospheric mood, as in this project drawing.

Another way of using light and dark tones to create interesting pictures is through the use of "counterchange"—placing light shapes against dark, and dark shapes against light. In this picture, the head of the lighter swan is placed against the dark tone of the reflection of the bridge, while the darker swan is silhouetted against the bright reflection on the water, and the white house is placed against a background of dark trees. These rhythmic patterns of light and dark encourage the eye to explore the image.

◄ SETTING THE SCENE

Using a stick of dark brown conté crayon, the composition is sketched out onto a sheet of pale orange pastel paper. Areas of the paper will be left untouched in the finished drawing, and these will serve to create the highlights. The warm color of the paper also contributes to the atmosphere of soft evening light.

▼ LINEAR DETAILS

A sharp corner of conté crayon is used to strengthen the linear details on the bridge and the house. The ripples and broken reflections on the water are drawn with a series of quick, calligraphic marks.

◄ MID-TONES

The mid-tones are blocked in using a short piece of conté crayon on its side. The image is gradually developed as areas of tone rather than using any hard outlines.

The image is refined with
further side strokes, for
example indicating the trees in
the background with short,
staccato marks. A white conté
crayon is used to heighten the
lightest areas on the house
and the swans. The rough
texture of the pastel paper
breaks up the marks in a
pleasing way, adding textural
interest to the overall drawing.

◀ DARK TONES

Gradually the darker tones
are built up, working
"negatively" around the areas
which are to be left as
highlights.

SEAS & COASTS

Seascapes are an endlessly fascinating subject, because there are so many different aspects to explore. You can choose to portray the wide-open spaces of sea and sky, or home in on an individual area of interest, such as a solitary boat or a small "still-life" group of seashells and driftwood. Alternatively, you might prefer to capture the human activity of beaches, boats, harbors, piers and jetties in summertime. Whatever your area of interest, you will never be short of inspiration!

The most important aspect is deciding on the viewpoint and composition. If you look straight out to sea with the shoreline and horizon crossing the picture plane horizontally, this can present you with compositional problems; what originally appeared to you as a wonderful panorama can easily appear deadly boring in a drawing! For this reason, it is important to position the horizon line carefully—it should not be directly in the middle, because this cuts the picture in half and creates a monotonous and dull composition.

If you want to emphasize the ocean, place the horizon line near the top of the picture; if you want to emphasize a dramatic sky, place the horizon line near the bottom. You may find that it is better to position yourself so that you are looking along the shoreline, with the beach and the ocean forming diagonals that recede into the distance. This will give you a much greater feeling of depth and space.

Seascapes often contain large areas of "empty" space, so it is important to include something—a rock, a boat, or a figure, for example—that forms a focal point and stops the eye from wandering off

◀ AERIAL PERSPECTIVE
Keep the effects of aerial perspective in mind when drawing coastal subjects; reduce tone and detail as the shapes of rocks and cliffs gradually move back in space. The exception to this is the sea itself, which appears darker on the horizon.

▶ THE HUMAN ELEMENT
This brush-and-ink sketch captures the atmosphere of the beach in midsummer. The figures are drawn with quick, "shorthand" marks that lend a sense of movement and animation to the drawing.

◀ DRAWING BOATS

Boats aren't easy to draw because of their complicated shapes, but they are attractive and will add interest to your seascapes. Make lots of quick sketches, recording as much information as you can.

the picture. Use the shapes of clouds, rocks and waves to create rhythmic lines that lead the eye around the picture towards the focal point.

Try to include something that will break up the horizontals in some way—perhaps a figure group standing on the beach, or boats in the distance that provide a link between sea and sky. Features such as these also lend a sense of scale, their small size emphasizing the vastness of the sea and sky. Boats on a rough sea toss and roll in different directions, and by positioning them at slight angles you can give a feeling of movement to the water.

It is best to avoid indicating the horizon by using a hard, straight line, because this looks unnatural, even when you depict a stormy sea. The atmosphere

▲ UNUSUAL VIEWS

The beach is brimming with interesting subjects, like this row of deck-chairs. Notice how the repeated pattern of stripes on the deck-chairs is echoed in the posts on the wooden pier.

out to sea tends to be hazy, particularly on a sunny, hot day, and the sea and sky merge into each other subtly in the distance.

Observe tonal changes carefully—the angle of sunlight, cloud shadows and changing water depth all create patterns of light and dark which help break up the large horizontal shape of the water and provide a sense of recession and movement. Careful observation pays dividends and helps you capture the very different atmospheres of the sea.

◄ BACKGROUND INTEREST

Here the composition is divided into three horizontal bands—sky, land, and sea—enlivened by the shapes of the hills and the cluster of buildings in the distance.

► OBSERVATION

Spend time watching the ocean. Understand how waves break, and how they contain specific areas of darkness and light. In this charcoal sketch the drama of the crashing white surf is accentuated by the dark tone of the cliffs.

▼ CLIFFS & ROCKS

Treat cliffs and rocks as simple shapes initially, then break them down into smaller shapes and add details such as vegetation and strata lines. Note the light and shadowy sides of the cliffs and build up the tones with hatched and crosshatched lines of differing density. Vary the direction of your strokes to emphasize changes of plane.

Harbor scenes feature every element of landscape painting in one image—land, sky, and water, as well as the bustling activity of boats, buildings, and people. Walk around the harbor with your sketchbook and viewfinder, and try looking at the same scene from several different viewpoints. When drawing, try to "edit out" superfluous details and concentrate only on those aspects which really interest you.

Colored pencils are used for this project. They are ideal for outdoor sketching because they combine the speed and linear quality of ordinary pencils with the added bonus of color. The image is built up from light to dark using hatching and crosshatching. Simply by varying the density of the lines it is possible to achieve a wide range of tones. Subtle color effects can be successfully obtained by interweaving strokes of different colors.

▶ THE SKELETON

The composition is carefully outlined with an HB pencil. It is worth taking time to get this right—it is the "skeleton" holding the picture together.

▼ HATCHED STROKES

The local colors of the houses, boats, sky, and water are lightly indicated using hatched strokes. The variety of vertical and horizontal strokes enlivens the image—notice, for example, that the sky is blocked in with vertical strokes, to contrast with the horizontal strokes in the water.

▶ PERSPECTIVE

Diagonal lines are laid over the vertical ones in the upper part of the sky using a warmer blue. This gradual shift from warm to cool blue gives the illusion of the sky receding towards the horizon.

42

▲ TONE & COLOR

The tones and colors are gradually built up by using closely spaced parallel strokes, changing the angle and density for different areas to indicate form. The finished image is bright and colorful, but the colors are carefully controlled; notice, for example, how touches of similar colors are repeated throughout the image to create a harmonious effect.

▲ REFLECTIONS

The boats' reflections in the water form a "mirror" image which helps stabilize the lower half of the picture. These reflections on the rippling surface of the water are carefully observed—notice that they are slightly darker in tone than the boats themselves.

GATHERING INFORMATION

When making sketchbook studies, record information on individual colors, tones, and textures, as well as making an overall view. Here, the artist has recorded the entire subject and then added individual details such as the patterns of the tiles and colors of the roof and bricks.

BUILDINGS

Although buildings are sometimes relegated to being minor features in a landscape, they are a fascinating subject in their own right and provide marvelous opportunities to develop your observation and mark-making. In any city, town, or village, the sheer variety of styles, colors, and patterns used in buildings provides a wealth of challenges for the artist and encourages him or her to use different media to achieve greatly varied results.

In particular, buildings offer a good opportunity to find ways of describing different surfaces and textures and the detail of complex structures and ornamentation. A sketchbook is as important an aid in drawing buildings as it is in drawing landscapes. It is the best place for making studies of a subject, which can then be used for a more considered drawing or painting back home, where you will have all your material in one place. You should make an overall drawing of the subject and record information on individual features such as doors and windows, together with the structure of any complicated areas and details. If you feel that you haven't gotten the best out of a subject, make as many sketches as necessary to capture the effect you want. Don't allow yourself to be distracted by people who come and stare at what you are doing.

The example illustrated on the opposite page is well worth following. Around his sketch of the buildings, the artist has carefully recorded, starting from the top left-hand corner and proceeding clockwise around the page, a color study of the light reflected in the windows in the main roof, a tonal sketch of nearby roof tiles, color notes for the wall of one of the houses, a tonal sketch of tiles along the roof peak, a compositional sketch of the whole complex in three tones, a detailed study of the pattern of the tiles on the roof in the right foreground, a color study of roof tiles in the center foreground, finishing with a tonal sketch of the shadow area on the left of his drawing.

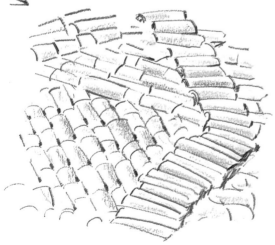

Architectural details can be as interesting to draw as whole buildings. Instead of trying to draw an accurate version of the building you see in front of you, think in terms of combining different types of marks to describe its individual character.

The quality of any type of line or mark is strongly influenced by the texture of the paper and the way in which it interacts with the drawing tool used. If you are using a soft medium, such as soft pencils, charcoal or brushes, which all "give" under pressure, you can get great variation in the thickness of the line produced. Hard pencils and technical drawing pens cannot be varied to the same degree. Light pressure will produce a light-toned line, whereas heavy pressure will produce a darker-toned line. Heavy pressure used with a soft medium or drawing tool will also create a thicker line, because the medium broadens under pressure. By increasing the pressure you apply when producing broader, darker lines, you can suggest shadow areas or heaviness. Lines that vary fairly strongly in tone and thickness can describe tonal changes and a sense of the three-dimensional in the subject. Finer, more resistant materials are better suited to more detailed work; soft, giving materials are best suited to a much broader approach.

VARYING THE LINE

Pen and ink can be used to produce a wide variety of marks (left). The nib of a mapping pen holds less ink than that of a technical drawing pen and cannot make such long lines, but its greater flexibility enables it to produce strokes that can vary considerably in width. Contrast these with the broad impressionistic strokes of a conté crayon that make up the sketch of the windmill (below).

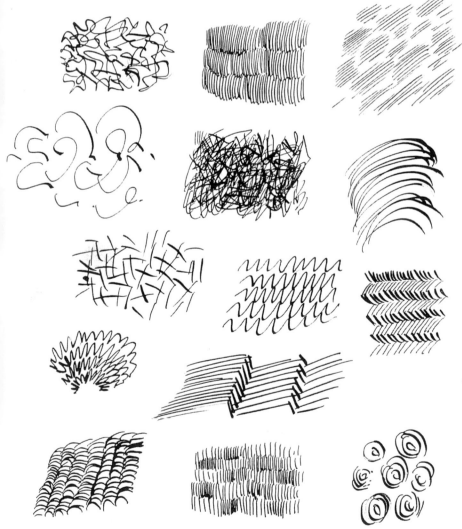

COMBINING MARKS

When looking at the materials and details of buildings, think in terms of combining different types of marks to describe their shape, form, pattern and texture. A close study of this drawing of a clock tower reveals the wide variety of marks used by the artist. As you can see, the potential artistic effects of pen and ink varies considerably.

An architectural drawing of this kind gives you the chance to find ways of describing different surfaces and textures—brick, grass, rubble, and foliage, for instance—through the way you make marks with pen and ink. You can use different pen nibs to create varied directional marks, and the amount of pressure you apply will increase your options.

Before attempting this project, practice making marks like those used here—straight, scribbly, curved, parallel, multi-directional, curling, circular, free, and closely hatched and controlled. Try to use as many of these as possible in the drawing: straight marks for the standing walls, more irregular ones for the crumbling and fallen brickwork, dense ones for the foliage, and lighter scribbly ones for the grass in the foreground and where the path and hedge lead away from the building to the right.

Make sure the brickwork follows the lines and rules of linear perspective (see page 16), particularly where the walls of the tower meet, and use different weights of hatching and crosshatching to create light and dark tones, without overworking them.

▶ PLANES & SHADOWS

Different planes – the front and side of the building and roof—can be mapped out with different patterns of hatching and crosshatching. Practice building up the hatching fairly heavily on the sides that are in shadow, without trying to fill them in completely in a pure black solid mass.

▲ FOLIAGE & GRASS

Make scribbly marks that vary in weight and width, using a mapping pen, to describe the different textures you see in the foliage and grass.

▶ TEXTURE & FORM

You can plot even complex areas of changing forms, planes and textures through the juxtaposition of different types of marks.

48

▲ OBSERVATION

A drawing as complex and skilful as this one needs to be built up in stages and is the result of careful observation of both structure and surface detail.

◄ CONTRASTS

Even in the darkest areas of tone, don't allow the crosshatching to become solid. If you make sure that touches of white paper continue to show through, they will create depth in the shadow areas and add a luminous quality. The contrast between these hatched areas and the white of the unmarked paper brings pen-and-ink drawings to life.

CITIES & TOWNS

Most people nowadays live in suburbs, towns, or cities, and buildings and streets make a readily accessible subject for the study of shape, form, texture, pattern, and perspective. Remember, you don't have to look far for inspiration; an ordinary suburban street can offer just as many possibilities as a large city square, and a small architectural detail or a single façade can be just as fascinating as a grand, sweeping panorama.

The thought of sketching and drawing in a busy street in full view of passers-by can be daunting at first, but once you get started it is always easier than you expect. With a small sketchbook and a pencil you can tuck yourself into a doorway and work without attracting unwanted attention from curious onlookers. Start with a simple subject, maybe just a simple façade, and avoid over-ambitious projects until you are confident in your drawing abilities.

An understanding of the rules of linear perspective (see page 16) is obviously useful when tackle this subject, but what matters most is your ability to observe your subject and interpret it in a way that is unique to you. It is important, therefore, to choose the appropriate materials and techniques to express what you want to say about your subject. If your interest lies in architectural detail, you will probably choose a linear medium such as pen and

◄ ATMOSPHERE

This lively sketch captures the hustle and bustle of city life. Pen and ink lines are overlaid with loose watercolor washes to give an impression of color and movement. Notice how the figures in the foreground accentuate the scale of the skyscrapers in the background.

▲ PATTERN

Using black ink and a broad-nibbed dip pen, the artist has concentrated here on depicting the wealth of detail and pattern found in a row of suburban houses.

▶ UNUSUAL VIEWS

Be on the lookout for unusual viewpoints. This steep, winding hill affords an unusual perspective that makes for a dynamic composition.

◀ SCALE & PERSPECTIVE

All the horizontal lines of the buildings and street converge at a point on the horizon known as the "vanishing point". The relative sizes of the people and objects convey their distance.

▼ DETAILS

Develop an observant eye for those small details that capture the spirit of a particular town or city—such as this old ornamental lamppost. The artist used brush and ink on smooth paper to depict its intricate forms.

▲ PARKS & GARDENS

The urban environment is full of interesting contrasts that you can explore in your drawings. In this city park, for example, the angular shapes of the skyscrapers form a backdrop to the natural shapes of trees, lawns, and people.

▶ CITY STREETS

A view from an upper-story window can give you exciting compositions, such as this traffic jam stretching far into the distance.

ink to produce fine, precise lines that describe every detail of roofs, windows, and doors. If you are more interested in capturing the busy atmosphere of a city street, or a particular quality of light on the buildings, you would use a broader, more fluid medium such as charcoal or brush and ink to create an impressionistic effect. As always, don't be afraid to experiment to find exactly what you want.

To render the solid, three-dimensional appearance of architectural subjects, it helps if you can find a corner of a street so that two sides of the building are visible rather than one. In addition, the oblique lines of the street create a feeling of depth and recession and lend added interest to the composition. Strong contrasts of light and shadow also accentuate the form and volume of buildings. A building seen at noon may look flat and uninteresting because the sun is directly overhead and casts very little shadow. In the early morning and late afternoon, however, the low sun casts long, slanting shadows that help describe the different planes of the building and pick out its features. In addition, these shadows provide strong contrasts of tone and color.

PROJECT: STREET SCENE

The combination of pen and ink and watercolor washes gives you the opportunity to capture the mood of a busy scene and the interplay of heavy shadow and bright sunshine.

Find a position where you can work undisturbed, and look out for interesting patterns of light and shadow on the buildings and across the street. The strong light from one side of the scene here created such a pattern. Establish your eye level in relation to the buildings, and then place the people where you see interesting groups.

Make a line drawing of the scene, using pencil or ink, or roughing out in pencil and then going over it in ink. Put in all the main elements and as much detail as you wish; work as quickly as you can, and draw the figures freely, concentrating on capturing groups rather than individuals.

When adding the washes, use a maximum of three or four colors; dilute them for lighter tones, and mix them for grays. Don't attempt to fill in the line drawing, but apply the washes to map out the broad areas of light and shadow that you see, independent of the details of the line drawing. Leave the paper white to show the lightest areas of all.

◀ PERSPECTIVE

All the perspective lines—in the buildings, the sidewalks, and the overhead cables—lead to a vanishing point that is set fairly low in the drawing. The low viewpoint increases the sense of tall buildings looming above the figures.

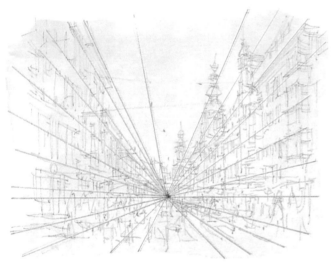

▶ LINE DRAWING

First, create the line drawing, using pencil and pen and ink. At this stage quite a lot of detail has been suggested, and it could actually stand as a finished drawing in its own right. However, it does not provide any suggestion of the effects of light and shadow, which will only come when you add the final watercolor washes.

▲ ORNAMENTATION

Heavy ornamentation on the building has been suggested, but no attempt has been made to put in any of the details.

PALETTE

COBALT BLUE

CADMIUM YELLOW

CADMIUM RED LIGHT

VIRIDIAN

▲ APPLYING WASHES

Use washes to describe large areas of light and shadow. Here, a cool green-gray was used for the shadows on the left-hand building, and warm yellow, gold, and orange colors for the sunlit buildings on the right-hand side.

The looseness of the image adds
to the sense of movement and
the shifting patterns of light
and shadow.

◄ FIGURES

Don't attempt to differentiate
individual figures, but indicate the
overall areas of light and shadow
that fall on them. Remember that
in a busy crowd, we see people as
groups or masses, and do not pick
out single figures.

CHAPTER 2
ANIMALS

The sheer variety of animal forms, their intricate textures and patterns, their character, their grace, beauty, and charm—all have been a source of visual inspiration since the first prehistoric artists scratched pictures on the walls of their caves. If you haven't tackled animals as a subject before, they may seem daunting at first. Unlike a human model, you can't ask an animal to "sit still while I finish off your nose"! By all means study photographs in books and magazines, but it is best not to copy from them; photographs tend to flatten form and reduce detail, and your finished drawing may, therefore, lack a sense of life and movement. It is probably better to start by making studies of stuffed specimens in a natural history museum. In this way you can examine at leisure the details of form, color, texture, and pattern. Making detailed studies at close range will help you to understand basic structures, such as the way a bird's wing and tail feathers lie and how the legs and feet are jointed. While you are absorbed in the act of observing and drawing, you are imprinting lots of valuable information firmly in your mind. This understanding of the appearance of the animal can then be put to use when you start to work directly from life, when the subject is moving too freely to be seen in much detail. You are then able to combine the lively impression gained from studying the creature in its natural habitat with an accurate rendering of its appearance and structure.

Contrary to belief, drawing animals does not require a textbook knowledge of anatomy; close observation, sensitivity and a basic awareness of form and structure will suffice—plus lots of patience and a willingness to practice, practice, practice! Continual watching and drawing will increase your understanding of animals and help you to draw them convincingly. Above all, never be discouraged if your first results are not successful. With practice both your observation and memory will improve and you will be able to tackle this subject with confidence.

MAKING SKETCHES

Good drawing is achieved with regular practice. Even experienced artists need to practice to keep their drawing from getting rusty. Often, the idea of sitting down in front of a subject with a sheet of crisp white paper can be intimidating, because you immediately feel pressured to produce a finished, perfect drawing. The result is that all too frequently you find it difficult to make even the first mark! Sketches, on the other hand, don't have to be perfect, or even finished, and no one is judging you on the results. They are your own private record of what you have seen and found interesting. Quick sketches can be complete in themselves; in fact, many would be spoiled by further work, losing the freshness of the first impression.

Keeping a sketchbook is an essential part of drawing and painting. Frequent observation and sketching will increase your understanding of the subject and help you record what you see more accurately. Get into the habit of carrying a sketchbook wherever you go, making on-the-spot sketches of anything interesting that catches your eye. A couple of pencils and a sketchbook with a hard cover for support, small enough to slip into your pocket, are all you need.

The problem with sketching animals is that they just won't keep still! So quickly get down as much as you can, and don't worry about producing highly polished images. Instead, concentrate on the overall shape and gesture of the animal. Then, if the animal hasn't moved away, you can add details and textures if you want to.

When you are sketching, use the drawing tools and materials that you feel most comfortable with. When you are involved with catching a particular movement or effect on paper, you don't want to waste time fumbling with bottles of ink or boxes of pastels when all you really need is a soft pencil! A felt-tip marker or an ordinary fountain pen filled with black or brown ink is marvelous for capturing the gestural rhythmic curves of an animal, and you can always moisten a finger and smudge areas where you want to add tone and shadow or bring out a form.

◀ ▲ QUICK ON THE DRAW

A lot of quick, two-minute impressions can be as valuable as a single, involved study, because they solidify your understanding of the overall structure and shapes of your subject. These sketches of rabbits were drawn with simple colored pencils in black and brown. If you sketch frequently, any stiffness in your drawing will soon disappear, and you will find it easier to express what you feel and see.

► MOVING IN CLOSE

The close-up study of a particular feature of an animal can provide you with a lot of useful information. Here the artist used conté crayons and colored pencils to model this tiger's head. A black waxy pencil was used over the top to reinforce the features and describe the pattern in the fur.

◄ SNAKES ALIVE

While this snake was basking in the sun, the artist took the opportunity to make a more detailed study of the wonderful pattern of markings on its skin. The snake's sinuous curves and spotted markings were quickly drawn with a dip pen and black Indian ink, then a fine watercolor brush was used to add the dark shadows. The background is also hinted at, placing the subject in context.

CAPTURING MOVEMENT

Movement is one of the most difficult yet fascinating aspects of portraying animals. Not only do different animals move in different ways, but the action changes as the animal increases speed or slows down. Before starting to draw a moving subject, spend some time observing it. Just sit and watch. Concentrate all your attention on the whole action and don't allow yourself to be distracted by details. Study the way in which the weight is shifted from one part of the body to another, and the way in which the angles between the different parts of the body change during the course of the movement.

Capturing movement by watching live animals can be difficult, because they often move too quickly for the human eye to follow. Photographs can be a useful source of reference, or you could play a wildlife video and "freeze-frame" a moving sequence at intervals and sketch what you see.

The lines and marks you make on the paper can be used to convey a sense of motion. Swift, light, flowing lines and broken, agitated lines suggest speed and energy, while thick, heavy lines give a feeling of stability. Vary the pressure on the pencil, pressing harder to emphasize curves and thrusts and lifting it slightly where the forms appear lost or blurred by movement. Avoid drawing a rigid outline of the animal—this freezes the movement. Keep your pencil moving all the time, hardly lifting it from the paper, using fast, scribbled lines and smudged tones to capture the essential gesture of the animal.

The way you position the animal within the picture area can also help to imply direction and motion. If the animal is depicted on the left of the picture, facing toward the right, and with more space in front of it than behind, the suggestion will be that the animal is coming into the picture.

▼ CATCH THE SPIRIT

This wonderful sketch expresses the sheer joy of a dog running along the beach! The artist used the side of a short piece of charcoal to block in a simple gestural outline of the dog, then smudged the outlines of the ears, tail, and legs to suggest rapid movement.

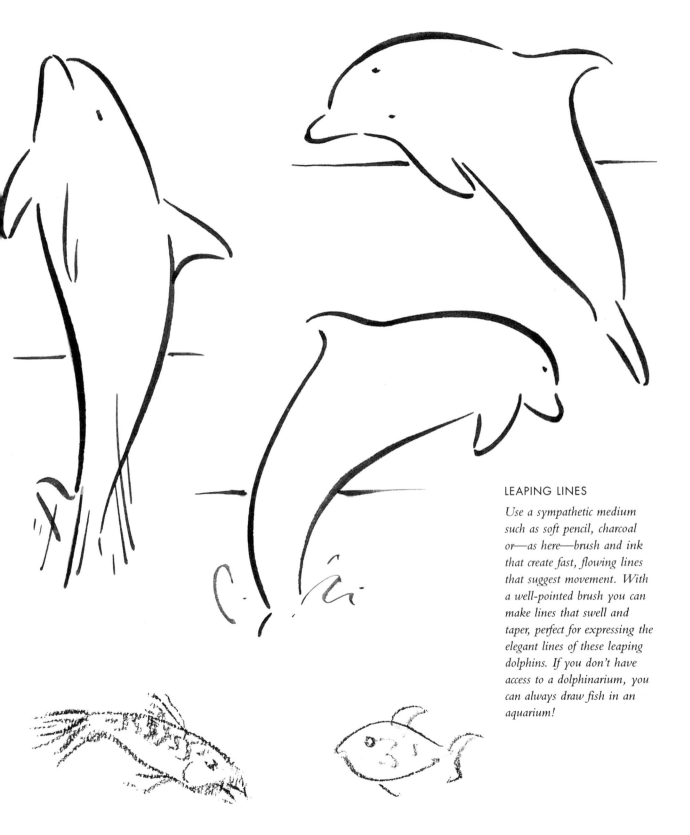

LEAPING LINES

Use a sympathetic medium such as soft pencil, charcoal or—as here—brush and ink that create fast, flowing lines that suggest movement. With a well-pointed brush you can make lines that swell and taper, perfect for expressing the elegant lines of these leaping dolphins. If you don't have access to a dolphinarium, you can always draw fish in an aquarium!

Whether it is a cat, dog, rabbit, or gerbil, your family pet is often your best and most cooperative model—especially when it's asleep or well fed and resting contentedly! Observe the animal carefully, and take note of how its body is "put together" Compare the proportions and angles of the various areas. For example, is the gap between the eyes equal to the width of one eye? Is the height of the back leg equal to the length of the back? You will need to work quickly as even a sleeping animal may suddenly change its position. Try to record the overall shape with a few confident strokes, ignoring all detail until you are satisfied that the proportions are correct. Leave the coat markings until last. Alternatively, make a series of small studies of details such as the eyes or paws. Once you are confident about drawing your pet in sitting or standing positions, you can move on to more interesting poses such as eating, stretching, grooming, or running.

Whereas different breeds of dog vary considerably in shape and proportion, cats share the same basic anatomy no matter what their breed (although the Siamese type is long and slender compared with Persians and domestic shorthairs). A cat's head is basically heart-shaped, and fairly small in relation to the rest of its body. On the average, the head should fit into the length of the body (excluding the tail) about four times. The ears are petal-shaped. The eyes may be round, oval, or almond-shaped, depending on the breed of cat. They are positioned roughly halfway between the tips of the ears and the chin. The cat's front legs are fairly straight, tapering down to the delicate forepaws. The hind legs, in contrast, have a "ham bone" shape.

The eyes are the most expressive feature of cats and dogs, so spend time studying and drawing them. In particular, look for the position of the highlight on the eyeball.

▲ OBSERVING PROPORTIONS

Compared with cats, dogs have well-defined foreheads and long snouts. The shape and size of the ears give a dog character and individuality. The position of the ears also conveys mood and expression—alertness, for example.

◀ BE QUICK ON THE DRAW

Keep your sketchbook and drawing tools close by, so that you can make quick studies whenever your pet takes an interesting pose. Using a fine-nibbed fountain pen, the artist here drew his Persian cat with a series of fast, curving strokes and created a believable likeness.

◀▶ SIMPLIFYING SHAPES

The structures and shapes of animals can be reduced to simple geometric forms—cubes, spheres, cylinders, and cones. The head can be represented as a single shape attached to the neck, which is, in turn, attached to the trunk. Constantly check the position of the limbs and the angles at which they meet the body. Once you have defined the main shapes you can start refining the forms and outlines and add details such as texture and coat markings.

TEXTURES

The colors and textures of fur, feathers, skin, and scales are an exciting challenge for the artist. When you draw animals, try to convey a sense of the soft fur of a kitten, or the rough coat of a terrier dog. Vary your marks and strokes according to the nature of the animal's coat; if it is rough and bristly, apply short, dark marks. If it's long and soft, make the strokes light and flowing. Try to choose the medium and technique that best interpret the texture and feel of the animal you are drawing. For example, if your subject is a litter of kittens, you will find powdery pastels perfect for their soft, fluffy fur. Or you could try drawing with ink or watercolor on damp paper—the lines will blur to give a soft, furry effect. Sharp lines can be added when the paper is dry, to give definition.

Your choice of medium will also depend on how you wish to interpret your subject. Short, stiff lines made with a hard pencil or a fine-nibbed pen are perfect for a detailed study of a bird's feathers; but if you want to capture a bird in flight you will find that charcoal, chalk, or line and wash have more flow and give a better sense of movement.

Exploit the qualities of different types of paper, too. Pastel, chalk, or charcoal used on a rough-grained paper will produce broken, textured lines and marks, while soft pencil can be blended on smooth paper to produce soft tones and textures. Tinted papers are excellent because their tone and color become an integral part of the drawing. For example, if you are making a pastel drawing of a lion or a tiger, a sand-colored paper provides a middle tone and shows through the final drawing, holding the other colors together.

As well as describing the outward appearance of an animal, the texture of its coat can reveal its underlying form. Observe how the direction of the hair, as well as any coat markings, follow the contours of the animal's body, helping describe its solidity. Pay attention to the shadows and highlights on the fur, which help describe the bone and muscle structure underneath. Picking out the areas of light and shade will help you build up an impression of form and volume. Use more densely spaced strokes in areas of shade, and looser, more open strokes where light is reflected.

Keep in mind that, to convey a sense of life and movement in your portraits, it is often better to hint at texture and pattern rather than describe every hair and feather. Too much attention to detail will make your subject look like a stuffed specimen instead of a living, breathing creature!

◀ SHAGGY DOG STORY

Be expressive with your mark-making to bring out the character of your animal subjects. Here the artist has used a compressed graphite stick to make a series of short, thick strokes that emphasize the shaggy coat of the dog to create an amusing portrait of his pet. If you've never used graphite sticks before, give them a try. They look like very thick pencil "leads" and come in various grades from hard to soft. They glide smoothly across the paper, allowing you to draw with boldness and speed.

◀ ▲
KITTEN SOFT

Conté chalks have been used here to bring out the soft, vulnerable nature of these tiny kittens. lines can be smudged at the edges of the image to create a blurred whisper of an outline.

◀ SCAREDY CAT

In complete contrast, this cat is trying to look intimidating; every hair on its body is raised. Here, a well-sharpened pastel pencil has been used to make sharp lines that delineate the cat's bristling fur.

Try to avoid starting with a definite outline of your subject as this can result in an image that appears stiff and lifeless. By merely indicating the position of the animal and then allowing the form and texture to grow from the inside out, you can create a lively and convincing drawing. The squirrel's tail in the drawing above, for example, is fine and soft. If the artist had drawn a definite outline, the tail would have appeared too solid, and would have lost its attractive fluffiness.

▲ BRIGHT-EYED & BUSHY-TAILED

There are no harsh outlines in this drawing. Instead, colored pencils have been used to effectively highlight the squirrel's red-brown coat. The contrasting background successfully draws attention to the outline of the squirrel, without sacrificing the softness of the fur.

◀ ▲ A PRICKLY SUBJECT

The spines on a hedgehog's back form a prickly barrier against attack. A fine-nibbed dip pen and black ink on smooth paper successfully capture the bristled effect with great clarity.

◀ ▼ BLACK & WHITE

The badger has a thick, coarse, hairy coat, the hairs of which radiate downward from the back. A soft (4B) pencil with a blunt tip was used for this sketch, because it gives strong, dark tones suitable for the badger's black stripe and paws.

When you are drawing animals, it is tempting to emphasize the features while underestimating the solid structure of the head and body. Try to think of your sheet of paper as a piece of clay from which you model form by "pushing" and "pulling" (exerting varying degrees of pressure on your pencil). For example, you will push back into the eye sockets, then pull out (applying less pressure) to develop the forehead and nose, and so on.

You'll find that the fur patterns and markings of animals give you a helping hand in describing the underlying anatomy. Hairs bend around shapes (that goes for spots, stripes, and patterns, too). They vary in length and thickness, depending on their location on the body or head. Practice drawing a curved shape and bending hairs around it. In this project drawing, notice how the artist renders the fur of the cat and dog by hatching with short, fine lines that follow the contours of the head and body. He varies the density of his pencil strokes to build up carefully graded tones that suggest a range of highlights and shadows.

When shading with pencils, always make your marks lightly at first, building up the tones from light to dark. There's plenty of time to make things heavier as you go along, and laying darker marks over lighter ones helps you to build up interesting textures.

◀ OUTLINES & PROPORTIONS

The outlines and features of the cat and dog are lightly sketched in with a soft (4B) pencil. The heads and bodies are first reduced to simple shapes (these can be refined as the drawing progresses). It is important to get the proportions of the subject right; light pencil lines are drawn in to help position the head in relation to the paws.

◀ LIGHT & SHADE

Areas of light and shade are assessed by observation. The shadows on the dog are blocked in using hatched lines; for the cat's fur, the side of the pencil lead is used to create smooth tones.

▲ TONES & HIGHLIGHTS

A softer pencil is used for creating the dark tones of the dog's eyes, mouth, and nose, leaving the highlights as white paper. The highlights on the eyes make them look rounded and full of expression.

◄ ▲ FORM & TEXTURE

The dark tones and middle tones are intensified with more hatching, leaving touches of white paper to suggest the highlights on the animals' fur. This gradual buildup of overlaid marks and lines helps give an impression of their solid, three-dimensional form as well as the texture of their fur.

FARMYARD ANIMALS

If you live in the country and there is a farm, nearby, you will find plenty of animals to draw there. Local agricultural markets and auctions are another good source of animal subjects. If you want to draw on a farm, remember to ask the farmer for permission first. Be careful not to frighten the animals by making loud noises or sudden movements.

Farm animals are generally more placid than wild animals. Horses, cows, sheep, and goats are willing and patient models, as they tend to stand still for long periods when grazing—though some of them do seem to enjoy moving away just when you are about to start drawing! Nevertheless, these animals are creatures of habit and tend to repeat characteristic movements. Cows in the corner of a field, for example, will often wander off and then come

▲ CHEWING THE CUD

Most farm animals, especially cows and sheep, will be inquisitive about your presence at first, but if you stay still and quiet they will get used to you and eventually will ignore you. This scene has been quickly sketched in using a 7B pencil.

back to the same position and continue munching grass. A good tactic is to work on several sketches at once, shifting from one to the other as the animal shifts and retakes certain positions. Start by sketching the basic shape quickly. Note the direction of the light and put in the shaded areas. Once you have this on paper, it doesn't matter too much if the animal moves, because you can continue the drawing once it has settled down again. This method may be frustrating at first, but gradually your reflexes will sharpen and you will learn how to capture the essential character of the animal you are portraying.

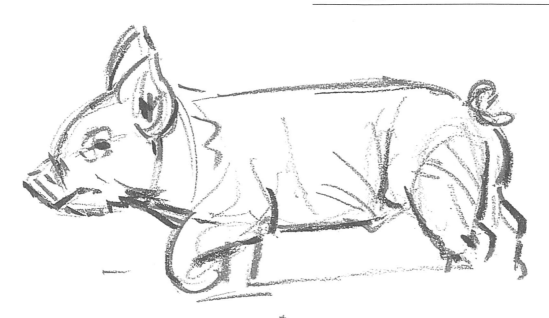

▲ ON THE TROT

The artist drew a rough outline as the pig was moving. Later, a more definite outline was drawn over the rough sketch, together with sharper details and shading. The effect is one of a pig in a hurry!

Explore various working methods to convey the character, texture, and movements of your subject. Think about the most appropriate medium for your subject. Smooth, blended tones, using the side of the pencil lead rather than the tip, will bring out the sleek, muscular build of a horse. Pastel is an appropriate medium for describing the woolly fleece of sheep, or you may prefer to use pen and ink to describe their curls with a mass of curved strokes and squiggles. Oil pastels make broad, expressive marks and have strong, bright colors, making them ideal for studies of hens and roosters.

◄ EARLY BIRD

A rough sketch was captured and then colored pencils used to represent the attractive plumage. Strong strokes of color successfully convey the texture of the feathers.

▲ CONVEYING MOOD

The artist used a conté crayon here to create an image of a powerful horse toiling away on the farm. The sketch is fairly dark overall, with the horse and figure drawn in rich, darker tones. The background is shaded, while details such as the furrows are emphasized with heavier color.

▼ AN OVERALL IMPRESSION

Pen and ink are ideal tools for drawing quickly "off the cuff". A flock of sheep will not stand stiffly at attention while you draw them. Because sheep are all very much alike in body shape, the artist used the same basic outline over and over again to build up the group.

PROJECT: ON THE FARM

There is no reason why you can't use your imagination and compose a picture by combining various sketches in one composition. This project drawing was made in just that way—the artist made sketches of the farm buildings, plus various groups of animals, and also took reference photographs. Back home, he had lots of fun making finished drawings from his reference sources and putting them together to make this lively barnyard scene.

When drawing groups of animals, it is important to get the scale right and to relate each animal to its companions. Look for points of reference. At what point does one animal's shape overlap another? How big is the gap between one animal and another? A head's length, or a body length? The relationship between members of a group is just as important as the proportions of each individual. Try to draw the group as a whole before you get down to the details of any one animal.

A SENSE OF SCALE

The farm buildings and animals are roughly sketched in using a soft colored pencil, making sure that the scale of the animals is correct in relation to their size and their position in the picture plane. Finer details can be added later.

◀ A SENSE OF DEPTH

A range of marks is used to describe the weathered textures on the old farm buildings. These, and the horse and foal, are drawn with cool browns and grays because they are in the background; too much color in this area would make the background jump forward and the feeling of depth in the picture would be lost.

▼ HIGHLIGHTS

Working over the whole picture, the depth and variety of color are gradually built up with a series of overlaid strokes. Little specks of white paper are allowed to show through, adding a touch of sparkle to the colors.

▲ CENTER STAGE

The pigs are the dominant feature of the whole picture, so they are drawn with the most attention to detail. Their rounded forms are emphasized by the direction of the pencil strokes.

▶ COMPOSITION

Stronger, bolder colors are built up over the whole picture, while making sure that the pigs remain a strong focus. The artist has successfully managed to capture a typical barnyard scene.

WILDLIFE

Nowadays, there are plenty of opportunities to watch wild creatures in their natural habitats. You can spot big game in safari parks and game reserves, or observe smaller native animals such as foxes and raccoons in the woods and on the riverbanks near your home. Working in the field, it is possible to make rapid sketches with the aid of powerful binoculars, telescopes, and cameras, which allow you to get much closer to animals and birds without disturbing them.

The zoo is an excellent location for animal sketching because it offers a chance to see, close up, a variety of animals not usually seen elsewhere. And there is a rich and varied source to draw from.

Zoo animals have cage habits—repeated behaviors that they have learned in captivity. The big cats, for example, with roaming instincts from the wild, tend to pace back and forth in a figure-of-eight pattern inside their cage. These repeated movements give you a chance to observe a given pose a number of times and get it down on paper quickly and accurately.

One of the problems with painting wild animals is that often they won't stand still long enough for you to make a drawing. Before you start, sit and watch your subject for a few minutes and try to gain an insight into its mood and behavior. Work quickly, on large sheets of paper, perhaps attempting several drawings at once. If the animal moves away, wait until it resumes the desired position and continue drawing. If it is eating or preening, your task will be easier as its movements will be more confined.

◀ ▲ CALL OF THE WILD
Drawing animals in their own surroundings and studying their behavior will add realism to your work. Before you start drawing, spend plenty of time just watching your subjects and observing their characteristic movements and gestures. Then quickly draw as much as you can from memory, simply concentrating on the basic form to begin with. The finer details can be added later.

▲ OUT OF FOCUS

A wild animal on the move is always exciting to look at. Here the spots on the cheetah's fur are blurred and the legs are almost lost, producing an impression of explosive speed.

▲ ▶ ON SAFARI

You may also consider using photographs as reference. To capture subjects that move too fast for the eye to follow, freezing a single "frame" in a wildlife video can provide the reference you need.

Making a detailed study of a bird or animal in isolation can be fascinating. But a drawing that sets an animal in its own environment, whether it's a cat sunning itself on a windowsill, cows in a field, or a bird on a branch, will add an extra ingredient and tell the viewer more about the animal. The project drawing shown here, for example, depicts a group of deer in their natural woodland environment.

The background may be very simple, with just a few lines or marks indicating leaves or grass, or even just a shadow on the ground. Alternatively, the background might be a strong feature of the drawing, showing the animal in relation to its natural habitat. Either way, it will place the animal in a meaningful context and add a sense of depth to the picture.

▲ SETTING THE SCENE

To start this composition, the main elements of the scene are simply and lightly sketched with fine charcoal on gray pastel paper.

▼ BUILDING UP COLOR

More subtle tones and colors are now introduced over the basic "underpainting" of the composition, and the deer's features are suggested.

▼ MORE COLOR & DETAIL

The main color areas are broadly mapped out using oil pastels. Concentrate on building up color and detail.

▲ FOLIAGE DETAILS

The branches of the oak tree are drawn with a dark brown oil pastel, and dots and dashes of light green suggest foliage.

▲ DAPPLED LIGHT

Strokes of various greens and yellows are swept across the grass to suggest the dappled light from the trees. The white markings on the foreground deer and fawn are dashed in, and a subtle white highlight, lightly smudged with a finger, is drawn around the edge of the right-hand deer to suggest reflected light coming from behind.

The main priority here is to draw the animal before it decides to move on. You can study the background separately, bringing the two together in the completed drawing. Make lots of reference sketches and use photographs to supply you with all the information you need.

Most artists prefer to treat the background impressionistically while rendering the animal in sharp focus; the background should enhance rather then compete with the drawing of the animal itself.

BIRDS

The biggest problem in drawing birds is that they are shy creatures, keeping themselves hidden. In addition, so many of them are patterned to blend into their environment for camouflage and protection—they can be difficult to spot, let alone draw! However, in order to draw birds successfully, you really must spend time observing them in their natural surroundings. Wild birds can be coaxed into your yard if you have a bird feeder, and while the birds are feeding and preening you have an excellent opportunity to sketch their movements and gestures, as well as their basic anatomy and the attractive patterns and distinctive markings on their feathers.

Alternatively, visit the aviary in your local zoo or park, where you will often find exotic and colorful birds on view. Here, the advantage is that you can study the birds' movements without worrying about them flying away! Any information you gather by direct observation can be supplemented by visits to museums and by referring to books. In the museum you will be able to draw from stuffed specimens and to study close-up details of wing markings, beak shapes, and so on.

▶ OBSERVATION

The shape of a particular bird's body, beak, neck, wings, claws, and tail varies according to its feeding habits and environment. Each bird is different, but what you need to look for is the attitude and stance of a particular species; compare the long-necked elegance of this heron with the short, squat shape of the kingfisher opposite, for example.

▲ LIFE & MOVEMENT

Birds feeding, preening, or just flapping their wings often make more interesting subjects than birds simply standing still. This rapid pencil sketch of a swan successfully expresses character, as well as a sense of imminent flight.

► COLORFUL SUBJECTS

Soft pastel was used here to block in the main color areas of this striking European kingfisher, with colored pencils used for the linear details.

Spend more time looking than drawing at first. Once you start to draw, work quickly, recording what you remember from the instant before (although birds sometimes remain in one position for several minutes giving you more time to check the accuracy of your drawing). Observe the overall shape of the bird; you'll find it helps to simplify the forms to basic geometric shapes—circles, ovals, and triangles—and lightly sketch this before adding the details of eyes, wings, and beak. Keep checking that the beak, legs and tail are in the right proportion to the rest of the body. A common mistake is to make the beak too large in relation to the size of the head. Other watchpoints are the eyes, which are often drawn too large, too widely spaced and too far back from the beak. Beware, too, of placing the feet too far forward under the body, making balancing on them impossible. Long

and careful observation of birds moving and at rest will help you avoid such mistakes.

When drawing birds "on the wing", the challenge lies in combining accuracy with spontaneity and a sense of movement. Sketching birds in flight is more challenging than recording them on the ground, but the finished results can be much more exciting. Once again, patient observation is the key to success. Study the birds' silhouettes against the sky, and limit yourself to a few quick, gestural strokes with your pencil or pen, perhaps adding a simple ink or watercolor wash to indicate the basic color and volume.

Try to record the birds in as many positions, and from as many different angles, as possible, all the time capturing what is essential and unique about that particular bird. Don't worry if some of your sketches remain unfinished—the most important thing is to capture your fleeting impressions.

◀ EXPRESSIVE MARKS
Here a simple, stylized sketch using brush and watercolor, effectively expresses the regal splendor of a soaring eagle.

▲ IMPRESSIONS

If you are lucky enough to live near a lake or wetland, you will
often see huge flocks of birds coming in to roost in the evening.
Even in the city you will see flocks of starlings in summer.
The effect is quite spectacular.

Drawing a single subject is fairly simple, but if you decide to draw a picture of several animals or birds in their natural habitat you will need to plan your picture as carefully as possible. Think about all the elements you want to include and exactly where you will place them within the boundaries of the edges of the paper. Try to arrange all these elements so that they create a balanced and pleasing image overall.

It is important, too, to create a feeling of movement and rhythm in your picture. Your aim should be to keep the viewer's eye entertained by encouraging it to keep moving around the picture from one area to another. Different shapes and sizes

add interest and variety to a picture. Overlapping objects will lead the viewer's eye naturally from one area to another. This technique helps hold the picture together instead of having unrelated bits here and there that don't appear to have anything to do with each other.

In the project picture, our eye is immediately attracted by the two large birds on the left-hand and right-hand sides of the picture. If we look first at the left-hand bird, the movement of the flock of flying birds guides our eye across to the darker bird on the right. From here, our eye is caught by the flock of birds situated on the rocks, most of whom are facing toward the left-hand bird. Thus our eye is continually guided back to the original source and back around the picture in a circular movement that generates a sense of energy and movement. The overall effect makes us feel actively involved in the picture.

Of course, exciting compositions like this seldom happen purely by accident, so before you get down to drawing your final picture be prepared to do a whole range of preliminary reference sketches. Time spent on composing the picture is well worth the effort in the end.

▲ PLACING THE HORIZON

The composition is drawn in lightly with a soft pencil before outlining the birds with a dip pen and waterproof black ink. Notice that the horizon is placed high up in the picture. It is best to avoid placing the horizon across the middle of the picture because this cuts the image in half and creates a somewhat boring and static composition.

▶ CROSSHATCHING

The hatched lines are worked over in the opposite direction to create a crosshatched effect. The seagulls are sketched in, ensuring that the shape and direction of the wings varies.

84

▲ APPLYING A WASH

A light wash of diluted ink, applied with a watercolor brush, is used to suggest clouds and to darken the ocean. The wash is darkened with more ink and applied to the darkest parts of the birds. Pen lines and a variety of squiggles add a sense of movement to the clouds and waves.

▶ CONTOUR & SHADOW

The rounded contours of the birds are established with loosely hatched pen-and-ink lines. The planes and shadows on the rocks are blocked in with the same method.

CHAPTER 3
PEOPLE

The human figure is perhaps the most challenging of all subjects to draw. Learning to render accurately the proportions of the figure, while at the same time instil a feeling of life and movement, is a real test of the artist's skill.

Contrary to belief, it is not essential to have a textbook knowledge of anatomy in order to draw figures. In the end, successful figure drawing depends on careful observation, concentration, and a willingness to keep practicing, even if your first attempts are unsuccessful.

One of the best ways to start drawing figures is to join a life class, where models are provided for you to study. Alternatively, ask members of your family, or friends, to be your models. Whether you are drawing a friend's portrait or making a study of a nude figure, you need to decide how your model will be posed because it is important that the outline of the figure creates an interesting composition. The word "pose" is perhaps misleading because it suggests a forced, artificial position. If your model feels self-conscious and uncomfortable, this will be reflected in the finished drawing and your unfortunate subject will look more like a tailor's dummy than a human being. Encourage your model to relax and move around freely; eventually he or she will instinctively take up a pose which is relaxed and natural.

If you prefer, you can even draw your models unposed, as they go about their normal activities: practicing a musical instrument, reading, doing the ironing, watching television, or even taking a nap. You could also consider drawing two people, or a group of people; the relationship between figures presents marvelous compositional possibilities. Use any props you can find in the house, such as curtains, cushions, and plants, to add interest and a splash of color.

Most important of all, get into the habit of carrying a sketchbook and sketching people whenever you can. There are countless opportunities to draw people unobserved: at the local park or the beach, where people are picnicking, walking dogs, or just relaxing in the sun; at street fairs, which are a riot of color and hustle and bustle; at sports events, in malls and restaurants; even on trains and buses.

FACIAL FEATURES

Before you can draw portraits successfully, you need to know how to draw the individual features of the face. These features are what make a person unique, and drawing them accurately is important if you want to achieve a convincing likeness. As you draw, observe your sitter's features in detail. Are the lips thin or full? How wide is the mouth in relation to the width of the face? What about the shape and thickness of the eyebrows?

SKETCHING EYES

Practice drawing eyes, watching for the subtle individual differences between the eyes of men, women, children, and older people. Observe, too, how the shape of the eyes can completely change depending on the person's expression and the angle of the head.

Spend some time studying and drawing individual eyes, mouths, ears, and noses. You will find plenty of models among your own family and friends, and you can draw them while they are reading or watching TV. You can also practice on yourself, using a mirror.

When we look at a person, we usually notice their eyes first. The eyes convey a person's personality and emotions more than any other facial feature. Eyes are easy to draw if you understand their underlying structure. The eye is a sphere, of which only a small part is exposed (think of it as a ball resting inside the round cup of the eye socket). A small portion of the iris (the colored area) is also hidden behind the eyelids.

Begin your drawing by lightly sketching the overall shape of the eyes with loose, feathered strokes (remember that a strong, hard outline gives the eyes a flat, "pasted-on" appearance). Then gradually build up the form of the eye and the area surrounding it at the same time, so that they blend together naturally.

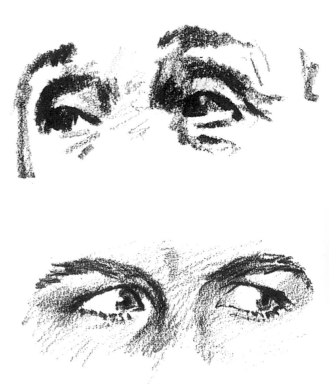

▶ LIGHT & SHADE

Highlights and subtle shading convey the spherical nature of the eyeballs.

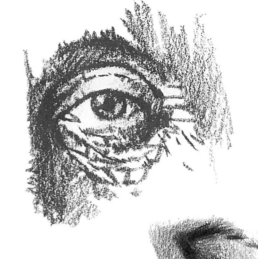

▼ EYES AT AN ANGLE

When the head is turned at an angle, the eyes may appear different in size and shape.

▼ ▶ CHILDREN'S EYES

Children's eyes are larger and rounder than adults' eyes, and bigger in proportion to the face.

You will notice that the shape of the eye comprises two semicircles, the upper one being slightly more curved than the lower. The eyelid casts a slight shadow onto the surface of the eyeball, and a shadow cast from the forehead accentuates the depth of the eye sockets. A dark, irregular line will give an impression of the eyelashes; never attempt to draw individual eyelashes—this creates an unnatural doll-like effect.

To capture the sparkle that gives life to the eyes you must carefully observe the various tones and highlights. In particular, look for the position of the brightest highlight, and leave that as a small area of white paper; it will really sparkle if you then tone down the whites of the eyes with subtle shading.

The mouth is second only to the eyes in expressing an individual's character and mood. A complex variety of delicate muscles around the mouth make it capable of an infinite range of shapes and expressions, and it is this mobility that makes it one of the most difficult features to draw convincingly. The most common mistake is to draw

ADULT MOUTHS

Mens' lips are usually thinner, flatter, and more elongated than womens' mouths, which are generally fuller and softer.

▼ **CHILDREN'S MOUTHS**

Children's mouths are small and soft, and the lips are much fuller than those of an adult.

the outline of the mouth first and then fill it in with color or shading; this gives the mouth a flat, pasted-on appearance. In order to capture the roundness and soft, mobile appearance of the lips it is best to avoid drawing a rigid outline and instead model the shapes using a range of tones. Finish by adding one or two crisp touches on the line between the lips.

The following general rules will help you draw mouths accurately and enable you to record the exact likeness of a particular mouth.

The upper lip is usually thinner and more defined than the lower lip, which is fuller and softer, especially in women and children. The bottom lip is also slightly shorter than the top one, and lighter in tone because it catches more light.

The nose protrudes from the face, but it has no definite outline; you have to model its form with light and shade. You will usually find a dark shadow at the base of the nose, and a lighter shadow down one side if the light is coming from the opposite side. Define the bridge of the nose with a highlight, and place a small dot of light at the tip. Pay attention also to the nostrils and "wings" of the nose, which are often drawn too small.

When you draw the ear, try to get a sense of its form emerging from the skull—rather than being stuck on as an afterthought! The complex whorls and curves of the ear may seem difficult at first, but frequent sketching practice will help. Generally, it is often best to draw the ears as simply as possible, avoiding overstatement.

▼ SMILING MOUTHS

An open, smiling mouth has a narrowed upper lip. It is unusual to see the bottom teeth exposed.

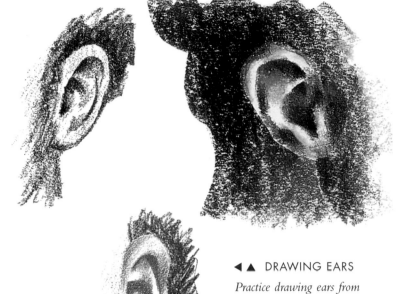

◀▲ DRAWING EARS

Practice drawing ears from different angles. Try to simplify the forms, concentrating on the major planes of light and dark.

◀▼ DRAWING THE NOSE

Build up the construction of the nose with hatched strokes, working progressively from the lightest tones to the darkest. The white of the paper is used for the highlights.

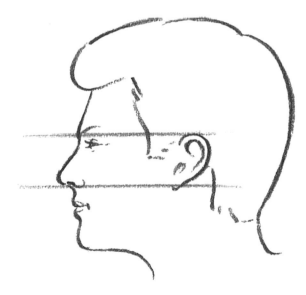

▲ POSITION OF THE EAR

From a side view, the top of the ear lines up with the eyebrow and the bottom lines up with the base of the nose. Its position is in the middle of the head—farther back from the face than you might actually think.

When you first set out to draw a complex form such as the human head it can be difficult to know just where to begin. It can be helpful to first visualize the head in terms of simple geometric shapes: the head and neck resemble an egg sitting on top of a cylinder. When viewed from the front, the "egg" is upright and fits more or less into a rectangle. Viewed from the side, the egg is tilted at an angle of roughly 45° and fits into a square.

Once you have established the shape and tilt of the head, you can position the features. Here you will find the "rule of halves" useful as a guideline. First divide the egg in half horizontally and then vertically. The vertical line acts as a guide for the position of the features on either side. The horizontal line marks the position of the eyes. Now divide the space between the top of the eyebrows and the bottom of the chin in half to find the position of the base of the nose. Finally, draw a line halfway between the nose line and the chin to establish the position of the lower lip. These

▼ MEASURING

The eye line is halfway between the top of the head and the base of the chin. A common mistake is to make the top half of the head much too short.

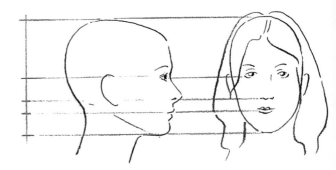

◄ HEAD PROPORTIONS

A knowledge of a few basic dimensions of the head and the way they are affected by the angle at which it is held will provide a sound basis for all drawings of heads.

◄ PROPORTIONS

Once you've established these proportions, assess where the hairline rests between the crown and the eyes, and where the tip of the nose and the line of the mouth fall between the eye socket and the chin.

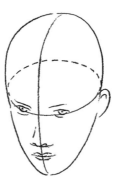

▲ EGG-SHAPED

The head is three-dimensional; think of it as being shaped like an egg. The eye line, for example, falls on an ellipse, not on a straight line.

▲ VOLUME

The basic volume of the head remains the same, regardless of the shape of the hair.

◀ CHILDREN'S HEADS

In babies and young children, the cranium and forehead are proportionately larger than those of an adult, and the facial features are set much closer together. The nose, mouth, and chin are tiny and soft, and the eyes are very large and bright.

▶ CAPTURING A LIKENESS

Getting the proportions of the head right, and the features in correct relation to each other, is important in capturing an individual likeness. Judge or measure the width of the head against its length. Other alignments to note are the tops of the ears in relation to the eyes, and the bottom of the ears to the tip of the nose or mouth.

measurements apply whether the head is viewed from the front or the side.

These "rules" of head proportion are based on the average person, who, of course, doesn't exist in real life! They are intended only as a guide, but they will enable you to see more easily the differences in proportion that distinguish one individual's head from another.

toward the top of the face. The top of the head almost disappears, and the curve of the chin is more pronounced. The ears now appear lower down than the eyes.

When a three-quarter turned face is viewed, the same principles of foreshortening apply, but this time in a horizontal instead of a vertical direction. When the head is turned to the side, more of the back of the head is revealed, and the features are aligned close to the far edge of the face. The edge of the nose, the far cheek, and the far eye are compressed closer together the farther the head is turned, and the tip of the nose may jut out beyond the cheek. Notice that the far eye appears slightly smaller and different in shape to the near eye. The distance from the nose to the back of the head is surprisingly long; it is a common mistake to "squash up" the back of the head.

▲ FORESHORTENED HEAD

Here the head is tilted back, completely changing the proportions. The features appear compressed toward the top of the head, and the nearer features appear much larger in relation to those that are farther away. Notice how the curved shape of the chin is accentuated.

ANGLED HEADS

Drawing the head from an angle—when it is tipped back or forward, or viewed from a three-quarter angle—involves careful observation and measuring. When the head is tilted downward, for example, foreshortening comes into play. The eyes, nose, and mouth appear compressed toward the bottom of the face, and the tip of the nose may overlap the mouth. The top of the head appears much larger, and the ears appear higher up than the eyes. With the head tilted back, the features appear compressed

▲ SEMIPROFILE VIEW

Although more difficult to draw, a three-quarter turned face can often make a more expressive portrait than a face viewed head-on. To get the features correctly aligned, use your pencil to compare the length to the width of the head and to check the angles and distances between the features.

PROJECT: PORTRAIT STUDY

The best approach to drawing the human head, if you haven't tackled this subject before, is to ignore the fact that it is a head and concentrate instead on analyzing the structure by the way it is revealed through light and dark tones. The head is a series of planes, some of which, like the nose, protrude, and some of which, like the eye sockets, recede. The forehead, cheeks, and chin, on the other hand, are gently curving surfaces. These planes and surfaces are revealed by light falling onto the head, so note the direction of the light and the way that surfaces facing it are lit, and those facing away are in shadow. Gradually build up the darker tones to the point where the form takes on shape and solidity.

There is no need to put in details such as eyelashes or individual hairs on eyebrows. The overall shape and proportions of the head, and the shapes of the eyes, nose, and mouth, are far more telling and convincing than the inclusion of unnecessary finer details.

The materials for this project are conté crayons in six tones ranging from white to very black, and a mid-toned, textured gray paper. Because of its

▲ LIGHT & SHADOW

Natural light from a nearby window throws one side of the head into light, the other into shadow for a dramatic effect.
The shadows cast on the wall behind the model help break up the picture space in an interesting way.

▶ CONTE CRAYONS

These are a traditional medium for portrait drawing. They are available in soft earth colors as well as the grays and blacks used here. They are a versatile medium; you can use the flat side of the crayon for shading and the tip for crisp lines and edges.

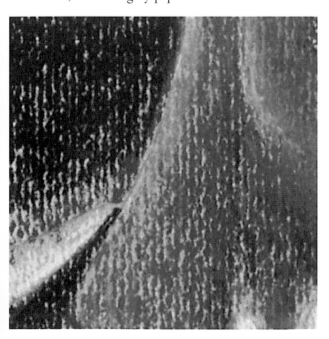

◀ DEFINITION

Often you will see areas of reflected light within a shadow. Here, for instance, the jawline and neck are defined with reflected light.

textured surface, the paper shows through the chalk marks across the drawing, and in places has been allowed to stand as a middle tone. The limited range of tones allows you to build up the image as simple blocks of tone, but they can also be laid over the top of each other and blended to provide smooth transitions from light to dark where necessary.

◀ ADDING LIGHT

The textured paper breaks through the overlaid marks, giving luminosity to what would otherwise be very dense areas of tone.

▶ THREE-DIMENSIONAL

The lightest lights and the darkest darks are contrasted in the face, the focal point. The strongly lit front of the head and the deeply shadowed side create a strong sense of three-dimensional form. Tones are treated as interlocking shapes.

▲ DEFINITION

The edge of the cheek is defined by the dark tone of the shadow behind it.

▶ BLENDING IN

The shape of the mouth has been carefully observed; it is viewed from a difficult angle in this pose. Subtle blending describes the fullness of the lips—notice the absence of a hard outline.

SKETCHING PEOPLE

Regular, quick sketching is vital to the development of your drawing skills. Even if you are out at work all day, there are bound to be times when it is possible to make a few sketches of people—may be on the train going home, or in a café at lunchtime. A sketchbook is ideal for working in public places, because you can work discreetly without attracting attention—a distinct advantage when you're sketching people, who can become very self-conscious or even annoyed when they realize that they're being sketched.

As an exercise, try making a series of rapid sketches of people. Don't worry about producing a perfect result, because you will be learning something very different from what you'd learn by completing a more detailed study. High-speed drawing forces you to identify the important facts and to appreciate the overall unity of the pose. You will also acquire a much better feel for the energy, rhythm and movement of the figure.

Start with 30-second sketches and then move on to one minute. You should be able to produce fairly developed and expressive studies. Next, move on to two-minute sketches. Once you're used to working quickly, this will seem like an acceptable time to set down what you see. The examples here show that it is possible to produce convincing figures in this short time.

ON THE BEACH

Carry a sketchbook and pencil with you as often as you can, and try to sketch every day if possible. There is no better way to improve your drawing skills and your powers of observation. The beach is a great place to sketch people in all kinds of different poses.

A RESPONSIVE MEDIUM

Drawing people unawares requires a responsive medium that will perform quickly and expressively. These sketches were drawn with a 9B pencil, which glides smoothly across the paper and readily produces tone as well as line. Don't be afraid to make changes and draw over the original marks— a contour composed of several lines can be very expressive. Erasing just wastes time and makes you more hesitant in your drawing.

PROPORTIONS

If you want your drawings of people to look realistic, you have to make sure you get all the different parts of the body in their correct proportions. This is easier said than done, since our eyes tend to mislead us into seeing some parts of the body as larger or smaller than they really are. It is all too easy, for example, to make the head much too big, or the legs and arms much too short.

The human body comes in all sorts of sizes and shapes. Luckily, whether a person is young or old, short or tall, fat or thin, there are some simple rules to help you get different parts of the body looking right and in proportion to each other.

The simplest way to draw figures accurately is by using the head as a unit of measurement. Allowing for slight differences from one person to another, the average adult human figure measures between seven-and-a-half and eight head lengths from top to bottom.

A child's body measures between five and six heads tall, depending on its age. In babies, the body measures roughly about three heads tall, and the legs should be drawn proportionately shorter.

▶ THE "IDEAL" FORM

Although no two people are exactly alike, it is helpful to memorize the proportions of the "ideal" figure shown here and keep these in mind as you draw.

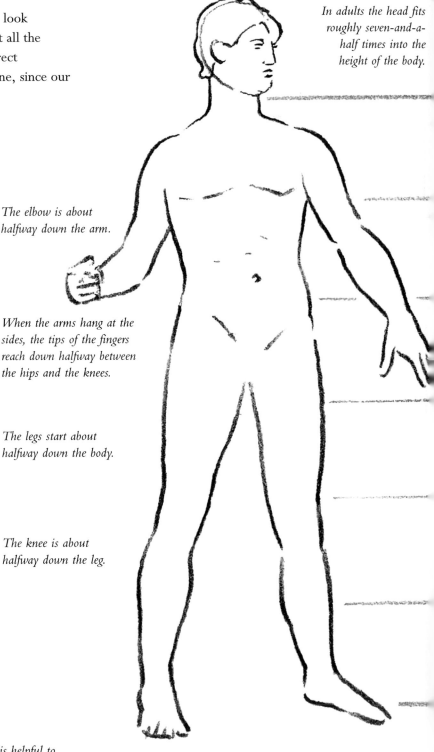

In adults the head fits roughly seven-and-a-half times into the height of the body.

The elbow is about halfway down the arm.

When the arms hang at the sides, the tips of the fingers reach down halfway between the hips and the knees.

The legs start about halfway down the body.

The knee is about halfway down the leg.

CHILDREN'S PROPORTIONS

The younger a person is, the bigger the head is in relation to the rest of the body. In babies the head goes about four times into the height of the body. In older children the head goes about six times into the height of the body.

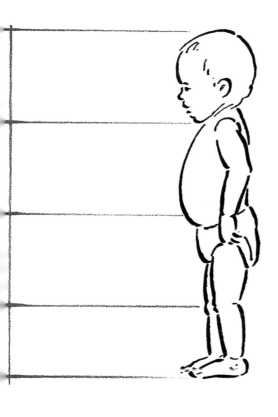

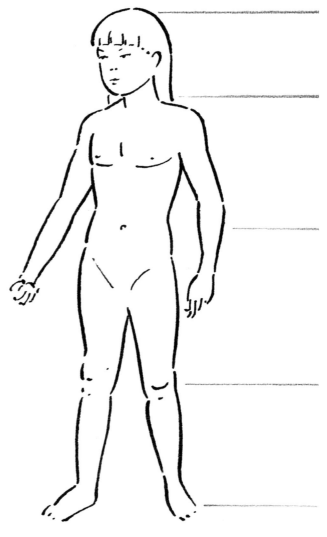

◀ FORESHORTENING

When a figure is seated or lying down, the limbs appear foreshortened. The shape of the body appears compressed and distorted, and some parts seem to disappear altogether. Try using the head as a unit of measurement for checking the proportions of a foreshortened figure. Here, the head goes about four times into the length of the body.

101

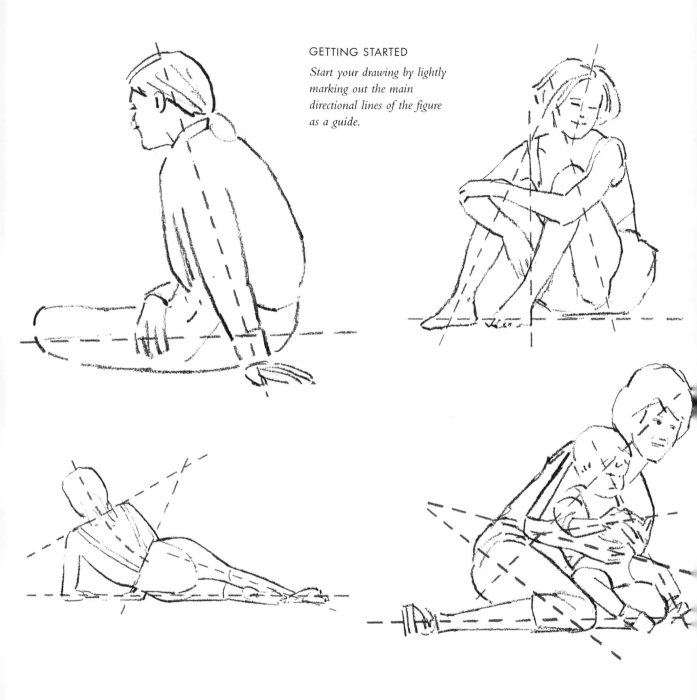

Start your drawing by lightly marking out the main directional lines of the figure as a guide.

The human body has flexibility and natural grace. Before you start to draw, spend some time observing your model and trying to understand the balance and weight distribution of the body in any given pose. This will help overcome any "woodenness" in your figure studies and make them appear convincing and lifelike.

Try using your pencil like a carpenter's level or plumb line to help you check the angles and proportions of the figure. For example, hold your pencil in front of you and line it up horizontally across the model's shoulders; then swing the pencil round until it aligns with the slope of the shoulders. Note in your mind's eye the angle between the shoulders and the horizontal of the pencil. Do the same with other horizontal axis lines,

▼ ASSESSING ANGLES

Look for the main angles and axis lines within the figure in relation to imagined horizontal and vertical lines. Drawing an imaginary horizontal or vertical line through the center of the figure will help you to see the variations in outline on either side.

▼ ▲ USING THE BACKGROUND

Use any features around the model that provide vertical or horizontal lines to help you assess the positions of head, torso, and limbs in relation to each other.

such as the eyes, hips, knees, and ankles. Similarly, try holding your pencil vertically and lining it up with the model's nose. Run your eyes down the pencil, noting the position and angle of the various parts of the body in relation to the vertical line of the pencil. It is surprising how wrong one's initial assessment of angles can be—you sometimes discover that a line that looks horizontal is actually at a slight angle. This type of discovery can help you get all of the rest of the drawing right.

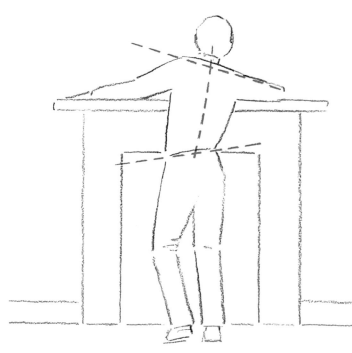

103

DRAWING A FIGURE

Conveying the solid, three-dimensional form of the human figure onto a two-dimensional sheet of paper is no mean feat, and it is tempting to try to solve the problem by drawing a solid outline and then filling it in with shading. Another trap we fall into is that of treating each part of the body—neck, shoulder, arm, hand—as a separate entity. It's little wonder that our completed figure drawings sometimes look more like cardboard cutouts than living, breathing people!

Think of the head, torso, and limbs as a series of interlocking shapes, each connecting with and emerging from the other.

The shape of the shoulders, for example, is affected by what the arms are doing, and a sideways tilt of the head is accompanied by a corresponding tension in the muscles of the neck.

To convey form and solidity, as well as the subtlety and grace of the human body, you have to think in terms of mass and volume as well as line. As you draw, keep switching from one to the other, feeling out the forms and "sculpting" them with your pencil. (You will find this easier if you draw on a large sheet of paper with a sympathetic medium such as charcoal or chalk.)

Draw the main contours with broad, free strokes, using your whole arm, not just your fingers, and use your drawing instrument sensitively to capture

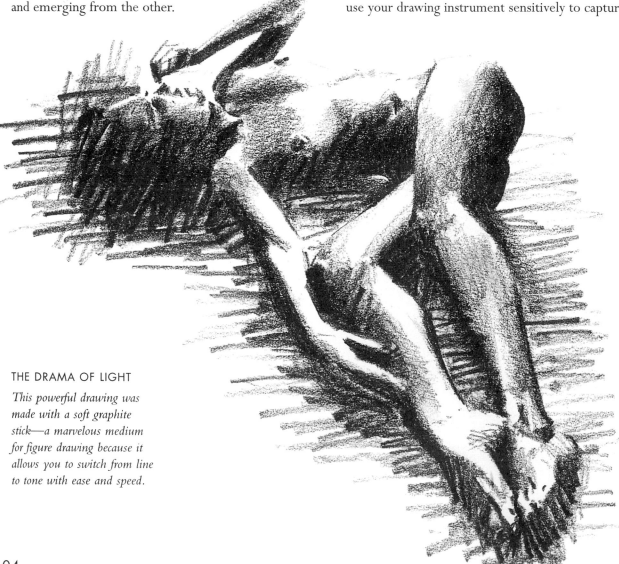

THE DRAMA OF LIGHT

This powerful drawing was made with a soft graphite stick—a marvelous medium for figure drawing because it allows you to switch from line to tone with ease and speed.

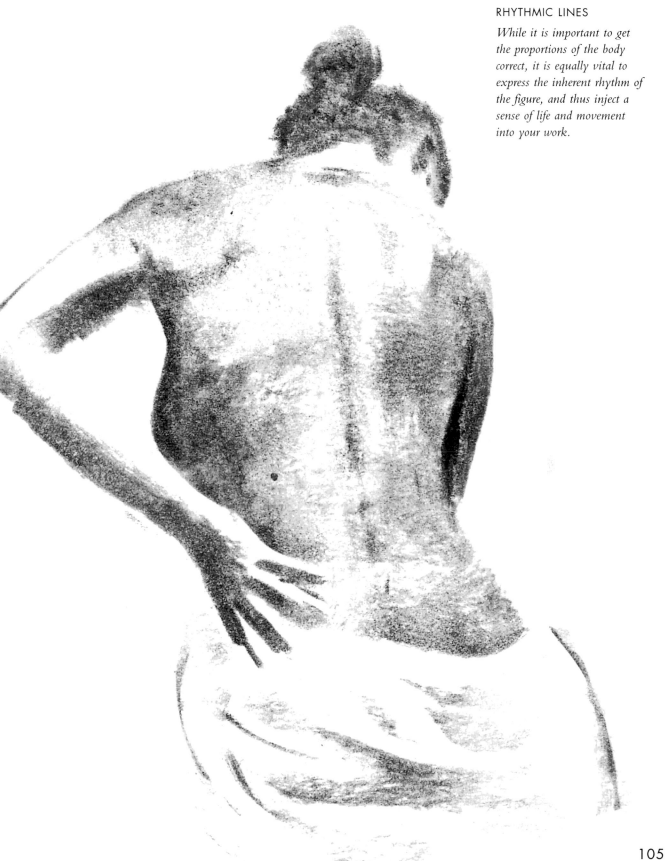

RHYTHMIC LINES

While it is important to get the proportions of the body correct, it is equally vital to express the inherent rhythm of the figure, and thus inject a sense of life and movement into your work.

▲ CLOTHED FIGURES

When drawing the clothed figure, you still need to be sensitive to the structure and form of the body beneath.

▶ STANDING FIGURES

An awareness of the rhythms and tensions of the body can help to overcome "woodenness" in your figure studies.

the rhythm of the pose. Try to "feel" each subtle change in the contour of the figure. Start with light, feathery strokes, and then gradually exert more and more pressure with your pencil to give emphasis to the "active" contours—an outthrust hip, the gentle curve of a calf muscle. Release the pressure slightly to make lighter, thinner marks for the "passive" contours—the inner curve of the waist or ankle. Keep moving around the figure, putting down the broad masses of light and shade at the same time as you draw the contours.

Always work from the general to the more specific, from the big shapes to the little ones. Your drawing should emerge gradually, almost the way a photographic image emerges in the developing tank: at first all you see are pale, blurred shapes, but gradually the image sharpens and becomes more and more recognizable.

PROJECT: THE YOUNG ARTIST

Children have a universal appeal and make a rewarding subject for a portrait study. They do, however, quickly become bored and fidgety if asked to pose, so the less formality involved in drawing them the better. Rather than ask the child to adopt a formal pose, you will often get more interesting results by simply seizing the opportunity to draw as it arises. A child absorbed in some activity, such as playing with a favorite toy, watching television or reading a book, will be much more likely to adopt a pose that is both natural and characteristic; the end result will be a lively portrait that expresses the individual personality of the child as well as providing a good likeness.

Before you embark on the portrait, it is a good idea to make several preliminary sketches of your sitter. This will give the child ample time to relax and settle down, and enables you to study his or her characteristic gestures and facial expressions. While you draw, keep the child amused and help him or her relax by playing some music, telling a story, or just chatting.

▲ SIMPLE SHAPES

The composition is lightly sketched out in soft pencil. The figure is broken down into simple shapes, and angles and proportions are checked.

▶ A TOUCH OF COLOR

The subject and background areas are blocked in with color, using the sides of the oil pastels. The colors are drifted on so as not to clog the tooth of the paper.

This project drawing has a refreshingly relaxed and informal feel. The little girl is absorbed in painting a picture (another artist in the making!) and her pose is spontaneous and natural. The drawing has been worked in oil pastels on a rough-surfaced white drawing paper; the pastel pigment catches on the "tooth" of the paper and leaves tiny speckles of white showing through, adding luminosity to the colors.

▲ FOCAL POINT

Most detail is concentrated on the child's face, since it is the focal point. The skin tones are delicately modeled with warm pinks and browns. Light is reflected upward onto the face, illuminating the nose, cheek, and chin. The hair is suggested with broad masses of light and shade, following the shape of the head. Then a few wispy strokes are all that is needed to suggest the shiny texture of the hair.

▲ HIGHLIGHTS

The colors are strengthened and the shadow areas indicated. The white of the paper is allowed to serve as the brightest highlights.

▶ SMALL DETAILS

The water jar is indicated with just a few brief strokes of blue, leaving white paper for the highlights.

▲ TONAL AREAS

The folds in the skirt are modeled with a series of darker tones. This artistic technique gives weight to the model and places her firmly on the seat.

▶ CHILD AT PLAY

The finished portrait captures the pose and expression of a child utterly absorbed in her activity—a wonderful childish attribute that deserts us as we grow older and more cynical.

MOVEMENT

Take your sketchbook to the local sports center, bowling alley, or swimming pool. Before you start to draw a moving figure, spend some time just observing your subject. While watching your subject, you will notice that certain phases or positions within the movement are more active than others. In a walking figure, for example, the point at which the leading foot is about to hit the ground and the other foot is about to lift is the peak moment of the action, and carries its own inherent momentum. If you can capture the peak moment in the stride of a walking or running figure, your figures will have energy and life.

Try to feel the overall rhythm of the figure's movement and understand how it works. It is a good idea to mimic the motion yourself in order to experience the way in which the balance of the body changes at different stages of the action.

◀ OFF-BALANCE

From the way the body is balanced in this drawing it is completely obvious that this figure is moving.

▲ FINGER DRAWING

Dip your finger into ink, powdered charcoal, or pastels and make fast, gestural drawings of figures in action. It's great fun and will help to loosen up your drawing arm.

When you feel ready, make some quick sketches. Use a soft, broad medium such as soft pencil, graphite stick, or charcoal. Try to capture the action in just a few lines. Sketch loosely, using fluid arm movements, and don't worry about detail. When mistakes and distortions occur, don't rub them out; leave them in and just draw the more accurate lines next to them. A single mark outlining a leg will make it look static, but a series of lines gives an impression of movement. Make fast, scribbled strokes that capture the rhythm and gesture of your subject as quickly as possible. Keep your pencil moving all the time,

BLURRING THE ACTION
Smudging and blurring parts of the drawing is an effective way to suggest fast movement.

hardly lifting it from the paper, freely following the action of the pose. As you sketch, you will find that you develop your own shorthand of quick strokes and lines that "catch the movement".

The types of lines and strokes you make in your drawing can also generate energy and achieve the desired impression of movement and action.

▲ A BUSY SCENE

How do you tackle a busy street scene full of people coming and going? First draw the setting, then add the figures. Establish the eye level and draw in the fixed elements. In order to draw the figures in the correct scale to each other and the scene as a whole, plot where their feet are in relation to doorways and sidewalks. Then sketch in the rest of the figures with their heads at eye level.

SPORTS

Swimming pools and tennis courts are good places to carefully observe and sketch people enjoying their favorite sport. Try to capture a particular stroke or action.

PROJECT: THE DANCER

When portraying moving figures, you will find it helpful to use a soft, sympathetic medium that encourages expressive, flowing lines. Charcoal, soft pencils, and graphite sticks are suitable for monochrome drawings, but if you want to work in color, then pastel is the ideal medium.

Pastels are extremely versatile in that they can be both a "drawing" and a "painting" medium. Just by twisting and turning the sticks, and using both the tips and the sides, you can create a wide range of effects. For example, working with the long side of the pastel creates broad, painting strokes that can be swept in as grainy "washes". Working with the tip of the crayon, or a broken edge, you can make thin lines and crisp strokes or rough dabs and dashes that

create an altogether different feel. It is possible to achieve a wide range of shades and tones using different techniques, such as hatching and crosshatching, and overlaying and blending colors.

Pastel papers come in a wide range of textures and colors. A well-selected paper contributes much to the overall effect of the finished picture, because some areas of the paper are usually left untouched, showing between the lines and strokes as well as around the borders of the subject. A rough-textured paper was chosen for this project drawing of a ballet dancer because it enhances the texture of the dancer's tutu.

▼ BUILDING UP DETAIL

The flesh tones and hair are filled in. Then the dress and headband are created with a cream pastel. For the dress, a piece of pastel is snapped off and used on its side, sweeping it lightly over the paper. The "tooth" of the paper shows through, suggesting the texture of the tulle skirt.

▲ CAPTURING THE POSE

The figure is lightly drawn with a dark brown pastel pencil. To capture the gesture of the pose, special attention is paid to the proportions and to the positioning of the head in relation to the arms and legs.

▲ CREATING A BACKGROUND

A suggestion of a background is sketched in with sweeping side strokes of a dark brown pastel to establish the figure in space. The strokes are "vignetted" off around the edges. The figure is modeled with a range of shadows and highlights, the tones and colors softly blended with the fingertip. Layers of color are built up on the dress.

▼ LAYERS OF COLOR

The fullness of the skirt is suggested by applying several thin layers of color, one on top of the other. Be careful not to clog up the grain of the paper and lose the texture.

▲ MOVEMENT

The hands are simplified and the fingers only vaguely suggested; the fingertips are blended into the background. This prevents the hands from looking wooden and gives a suggestion of movement.

◀ LIGHT & DARK

The head, half lost in shadow, is simply stated in terms of light and dark masses. The forms of the face, neck, shoulders, and arms are picked out with a few telling white highlights.

▶ GRACEFUL DANCER

The finished picture captures the grace and elegance of a dancer's movements, and the liveliness of the pastel strokes lends life and animation to the pose.

GROUPS

In some ways, drawing groups of people is easier than drawing single figures. If you are drawing people relaxing in a café or sunbathing on the beach, for instance, you can treat them quite broadly, concentrating on an overall impression rather than a detailed study. The most significant aspect is the relationship between the figures and the "story" they tell.

When tackling groups of figures, first draw them as one overall shape. Look for characteristic shapes and gestures and concentrate on the relationship between the "positive" shapes of the figures and the "negative" spaces between them, using both elements to define the figures and develop an interesting composition. Watch out for awkwardly placed hands, arms that hang limply, and heads that are all on the same level. You'll find that looking at the group through a viewfinder (see page 17) will bring these faults to your attention because distracting background details are cut out.

The overall directions within each figure (the

▲ INFORMAL GROUPS
This colorful pastel drawing conveys the easy familiarity of a family enjoying a picnic in the country.

▶ FORMAL GROUPS
The relaxed poses and smiling expressions help to lighten the feel of this more formally posed group.

angles of shoulders, arms and legs), the relative positions of one part to another (where the legs fall in relation to the shoulders) and the distribution of weight all need to be carefully observed to capture the specific poses of the figures (see pages 100–101).

Think of how you can use directional lines to follow through from one figure to the next to link them into an overall group. Emphasize the informal bond between a family group, for example, by placing the sitters close together, perhaps looking at each other, hands touching.

It is important to treat the figures and the background in the same style, continually working between the two and assessing one against the other. Once you are satisfied with the broad picture you can worry about individual hands, feet, and faces and begin to add the touches that differentiate one figure from another.

◀ OBSERVATION

The figures and background are drawn in, using a blue technical drawing pen with a fine nib. Despite the sketchiness of the drawing, the figures are carefully observed.

▲ ADDING A WASH

A watercolor wash of yellow ochre, diluted to a pale tone, is brushed over the paper while it is still damp.

◀ STRONG COLOR

A pink wash of acrylic paint (vermilion hue, diluted with water to a soft tone) is added across the background and foreground. Strong blues and blue-greens in acrylic are used to begin to define the forms of the figures. These stronger colors establish the figures in a nearer plane than the background.

Before you embark on a drawing, you need to step back and evaluate your subject, not only as a living person occupying three-dimensional space, but also as a flat pattern—a "jigsaw puzzle" of interlocking shapes, colors, and tones—that adds up to a balanced design. Ask yourself where to position the subject on the paper, how much space to leave around the subject, where the focal point of the picture will be, and how to guide the viewer's eye to that focal point. Remember that the background is not an empty area where nothing happens; it is an integral part of the "puzzle". The "negative" shapes around and behind the "positive" shape of the subject should be interesting and varied.

ACRYLIC

 PERMANENT MAGENTA

 VERMILION HUE

 WINSOR BLUE

 CADMIUM YELLOW

OIL PASTELS

 BURNT SIENNA

 FIR GREEN

 PRUSSIAN BLUE

 ORANGE

 YELLOW OCHRE

▲ OIL PASTELS

The cool colors in the figures are balanced by the warm earth reds on the bench. Touches of orange on the front of the bench help to pull it into the same plane as the nearer parts of the figures, whereas the duller colors on the back of the bench place it further back.

▼ HIGHLIGHT

Just one simple highlight has been added to emphasize the position of the figure leaning forward.

In this project the composition has been organized into three horizontal bands. The top band comprises a very simple background. In the middle band, strong, contrasting colors—blue and orange—have been used to focus attention on the figures. The bottom band provides a simple foreground broken up by the shapes of the men's feet and the pigeons. The top and bottom bands both form strong negative shapes around the central area, the whole image fusing together in a series of interlocking shapes.

This project explores the use of a variety of mixed media, with a technical pen used for the drawing, acrylic paints used to provide the foundation of warm and cool colors, and oil pastels used to add touches of bright color that lead the eye across the drawing.

▲ ANGLES

The heads of the three men are placed at different heights and angles. This serves to break up the horizontal line along the top of the bench. The background extends down between the figures to form strong negative shapes.

◄ BRIGHT COLOR

The horizontal lines of the bench are broken up by simple shapes described with bright colors. These colors provide interest right across the picture—although, because they gradually fade out toward the edges, they help concentrate full interest on to the figures.

▶ VISUAL LINKS

The pigeons are treated as linked shapes but are less strongly stated than the men's shoes. The feet and pigeons break up the horizontal line along the bottom of the bench, linking the middle and lower areas of the drawing.

▲ DEEP IN CONVERSATION

Some areas of the drawing are reinforced with more line work. The original background wash has been left to show as a light tone across the middle of the drawing, providing an effective foil for the blues and grays of the figures. The drawing was developed at home from rough drawings done on location, but the artist retained a spontaneous feel by working very quickly. Tonal and complementary contrasts are used here to draw the eye across the drawing.

CHAPTER 4
STILL LIFES & INTERIORS

There are obvious practical advantages in choosing to draw still lifes and interior scenes. You have none of the uncertainties of landscape painting, with its changing weather and light; you can choose the objects you want to draw and arrange them in any way you like; and you can even control the lighting by using strategically placed lamps and so on. And, provided you can set up your group where it won't be disturbed, you can study your subject at leisure—and in warmth and comfort!

No matter how little time you have, or how cramped you work space is, a still life can be set up in minutes and will offer endless possibilities for exploring composition, shapes and forms, surface textures, light and space.

It is unfortunate that the term 'still life' often brings to mind the somewhat staid and conventional set- up of wine bottles, fruit and a draped cloth that we remember from art classes. In fact, a still life can consist of anything you like: it could be a single flower in a jam jar, a plate of mushrooms, or a pair of sagging old boots. The main thing is that you should enjoy drawing your subject, so try to select objects that have some meaning for you, perhaps relating to a hobby or activity that you enjoy.

The best still lifes have some sort of theme, such as flowers and fruits, or vegetables and kitchenware, or potted plants and gardening equipment. Because these objects are related by association they naturally create a harmonious picture. Or the theme could be a purely visual one: if you enjoy rendering textures, for example, a group consisting of glass, wood, metal and fabric would provide plenty to get your teeth into. If it is shape and form that interest you, why not assemble a group of bowls, vases and bottles.

Whatever objects you choose, they will need to be arranged with care. Make sure that there is variety of color, tone, texture, shape, and size. Try to arrange interesting intervals of space between the objects, and let some items overlap others so that the eye is led from one area of the picture to another.

ARRANGING THE GROUP

Once you've selected an interesting group of objects, the next step is to put them together to arrive at a composition that is pleasing to the eye. If you haven't tackled this subject before, don't be tempted to include too much. Start with a simple arrangement of three or five objects (uneven numbers work better than even ones). Select the objects for their different qualities of shape, form, texture, tone, and color (if you are working in color). Place them on a tabletop so that they link and overlap; you want them to form a strong overall shape on the paper, such as a triangle, an oval, or an L-shape. Decide which object or area will be the focal point of the group, and make sure it is placed off-center and not in the middle. Place

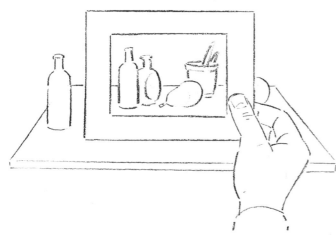

▲▼ VIEWING FRAME

Look at your still-life group through a viewfinder (see page 17), the edges act as a kind of picture frame. By moving it side to side, up and down, back and forth, you will discover many more potential compositions within a single subject. If you don't have a viewfinder, make one, using the same principles, with your fingers and thumbs.

▼ CROPPING IN

The subject can be framed in several different ways. Choose a particularly interesting area to concentrate on. By homing in on different parts of the group, it is possible to make several different drawings from one setup.

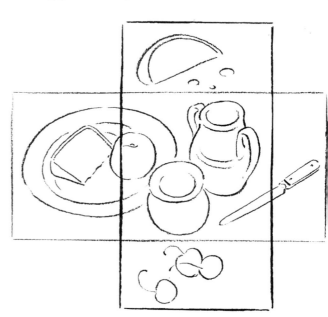

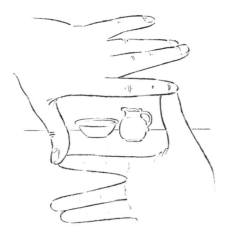

◀ VIEWPOINT

A high viewpoint, looking down on the group, can provide an unusual composition in which shapes are emphasized and space is flattened.

▼ ► POSITIVE & NEGATIVE SHAPES

A subject is made up of a series of shapes formed by the objects in the composition and by the spaces around them. Negative shapes are just as important as positive ones in creating a strong composition, and can be used to balance the main shapes within the drawing.

▲ SIMPLICITY

This composition is made up of a variety of simple interlocking shapes.

▲ BACKGROUNDS

The shape in the background defines the pitcher, and balances the bottle.

▲ BALANCE

The shapes formed by the table and window balance each other.

▼ DEFINITION

The background shape serves to define the bottle and balance the pitcher.

the setup close to its background, which could be a wall or even the corner of a room.

When you have made an arrangement that pleases you, move around the group and look at it from different angles and eye levels to see which makes the better composition. You will find a cardboard viewfinder (see page 17) useful here; when the subject is concentrated within the window of the frame, you can see at a glance any pitfalls in the composition. First frame the overall composition. Does it look boring? Try moving in closer on one area; you may find that homing in on a small section of the group results in a more interesting composition. Do several quick thumbnail sketches of the group, paying particular attention to the positive and negative shapes created by the objects, their relation to the background, and their position on the paper.

It is important that each individual element contributes to the total design. Try to see beyond the objects as "things"—a pitcher, an apple, and a plate—and look at your subject as a series of flat

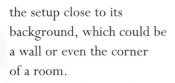

◄ KEEP IT SIMPLE

The simplest subjects often make the most eloquent drawings. Here, fine hatching with colored pencils is used in a detailed study of color, form, and texture.

▲ UNITY & VARIETY

A selection of bottles makes an intriguing still-life subject. Note how the shapes echo each other, creating unity and harmony, and how the bottles vary in shape, size, and height, avoiding monotony.

▶ NATURAL SHAPES

Nature has a lot to teach us about the art of composition. A group of seashells on the beach makes an unusual still life subject—and it's already arranged for you!

shapes, colors, tones, and patterns that link together, just like a jigsaw puzzle. Strong compositions have interesting negative as well as positive shapes; the "negative" shapes are those between and around the objects in the group, and are just as important as the "positive" shapes of the objects themselves. Remember, the background is as important as the main subject; introducing a patterned wallpaper, tablecloth, or draped fabric will break up flat surfaces.

A well-composed still life has both unity and variety. This may sound contradictory, but it makes sense: unity creates harmony, but too much

▲ ▶ THE INTERSECTION OF THIRDS

The traditional way to produce a balanced, satisfying composition is to use the "intersection of thirds". Just imagine your drawing paper divided into thirds, both horizontally and vertically; the intersection of the thirds produces four "ideal" points on which to position the main parts of your subject. The composition (above) is divided horizontally into thirds, and the cup and basket align with the vertical thirds. The flower vase and window frame (right) both align with the vertical thirds.

harmony creates monotony—which is why we also need variety! Unity is created by repeating or echoing shapes, tones, colors, directions, angles, and so on. To prevent visual boredom, we combine unity with variety and contrast. For example, a still life of fruits, bowls, and pitchers contains rounded shapes and forms, which gives unity. But if those objects vary in size, color, and tone, and if you introduce linear elements, such as a window frame in the background, you introduce variety and contrast, which keep the eye entertained.

Another aspect to consider is the lighting. The way in which light moves through the picture helps to give it a feeling of depth and three-dimensional space. Choose a single source of light, preferably coming from one side, because this creates a clear pattern of light and shadow that helps to explain forms. In addition, the shadows cast by the objects on to the table help to link everything together.

▲ OVERALL SHAPES

Think about the overall shape your still-life group will make on the paper. For example, these simple objects are carefully arranged to form an inverted triangle.

The objects in this project have been arranged to form a triangular shape, but the highest point is considerably off-center within the picture area. This creates an asymmetrical composition that is more dynamic than a symmetrical one in which the tip of the triangle is in the centre. The objects have been overlapped to create a variety of interesting shapes within the composition, and nothing stuck out on its own. The window in the corner balances the main subject, and fills what would otherwise be an awkward space.

Still-life drawings are more interesting if they have a theme, and the culinary theme of fruits, vegetables, and kitchen equipment has been a favorite throughout the history of art. For this project a few simple objects have been chosen which look "right" together and which contain enough variety of shape, size, and texture to keep the eye entertained.

You will need 2B, 4B, and 6B pencils, an eraser, and a sheet of drawing paper. Don't work too small; use a sheet large enough to allow you to move your arm freely as you draw.

First set up the subject. You could arrange objects similar to those here, or something different, as long as your group has an underlying theme. Place the objects on a tabletop so that they link and overlap to form a strong overall shape, such as the triangular one in this example. Place the setup close to its background, which could be a wall or the corner of a room, and avoid very strong light, since heavy shadows will conceal too much of the forms. Include a little of the background, but the still life

▼ DIMENSIONS

Once the composition is decided upon, the dimensions of the still-life group are lightly marked onto the paper using a 2B pencil, along with the position of the tabletop and the window. Then the positions and dimensions of each object are plotted in relation to the others. Try to do this by eye, or check by measuring with a pencil.

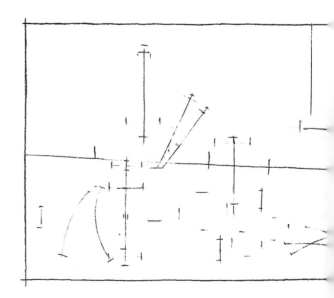

▲ DEVELOPING SHAPES

The shapes within the composition are built up by moving from one object to the next where they intercept each other, and noting both the shapes between objects and the shapes of the objects themselves. Keep reassessing the drawing, putting in changes without erasing the old lines.

itself should occupy most of the paper. As you arrange the objects, note the shapes between objects and those formed by the edges of the paper—the "negative" shapes—as well as the "positive" shapes of the objects themselves. Note also the shapes formed by the cast shadows: do they help create interesting rhythmic lines that link the objects together? Look for the best viewpoint, and adjust your position in relation to the group in order to find the best arrangement.

Begin by plotting the positions of the main objects in relation to each other, and put in the most

▲ BUILDING UP SURFACE

Areas of hatched lines are roughed in to indicate solid surface. Don't fill in whole areas with solid shading; work lightly and let the hatching follow the direction of different surfaces to describe changes of plane within an object.

▲ LIGHT HATCH MARKS

Areas facing away from the light source are built up with additional light hatching, using a softer, 4B pencil. The hatched lines don't have to stay strictly within the outlines of the shapes—your drawing will be livelier if you allow them to be loose and a little scribbly.

▶ CREATING SPACE

Where the edge of one surface or object passes behind another, break the line before it meets the object in front—this will suggest that there is a space between them. If the lines defining each object are drawn right up to each other, this will flatten the image.

▲ CHANGES OF DIRECTION

Let the hatching lines follow the direction of the surface being described, changing direction with any changes of plane. These changes of direction also make the image more lively and interesting to look at.

important background features. Then start on the main forms, noting where one object overlaps or intercepts another. You can then start to build up a sense of form and solidity and suggest the play of light on the objects.

There are various ways to develop this project further. You could make another drawing from a different viewpoint, studying the changed relationships between objects and the different way in which the light falls across the subject. Or you could take a high viewpoint, looking down on the

subject from above. Or you could create a more abstract composition by moving in close so that the setup completely fills the paper, and letting some of the objects around the edges of the group be cropped off at the edges of the paper.

▼ AVOIDING OUTLINES

There need not be a continuous, hard line around every shape or surface. It is more convincing to let edges come and go, losing the outline where there is a highlight, and finding it again in shadow areas or where you want to separate an object from what is behind it.

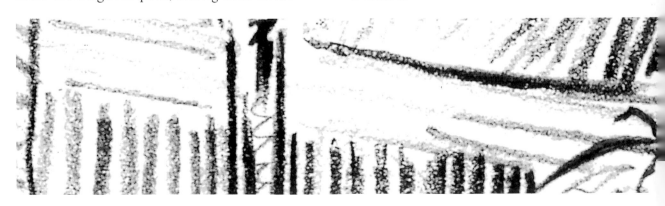

▲ FINISHING OFF

The drawing was completed by continuing to describe the surfaces facing away from the light using a soft, 6B pencil, and going over some of the areas previously worked with a lighter pencil. Even in the darkest areas some of the white paper has been allowed to shine through, giving the finished drawing sparkle and luminosity.

▶ WEIGHT & TONE

Combinations of lines drawn with pencils of different grades of softness enable you to vary the weight of the line and introduce tonal variety.

A chance arrangement of jewelry and tiny trinket boxes, casually strewn on a dressing table, forms the basis of this delicate conté drawing. A subject like this might easily be overlooked, unless you have your trusty and invaluable viewfinder close to hand.

"FOUND" GROUPS

The still life based on the chance find has a charm all of its own and is very different from the carefully composed grouping of specifically chosen objects. For the imaginative artist, a pair of old boots "still life," presenting fascinating problems of form and interpretation. A shirt hanging over the back of a chair offers the opportunity to study patterns of light and shadow created by its creases and folds; the kitchen table after breakfast, with its cups, plates, spoons, and so on, forms a refreshingly casual arrangement of related shapes; a heap of toys dropped by chance in the corner of a child's bedroom is a riot of color, shape, and pattern, ideal

for a study executed in bright pastels or colored pencils.

There are plenty of potential subjects outdoors as well as indoors: a pile of discarded flowerpots on the patio, a corner of the garden shed with gardening tools and a pile of onions, even a chance grouping of stones and pebbles on the beach, all of which serve as interesting still-life studies.

Good drawings spring not only from the beautiful

and the picturesque, but also from the small, the everyday, even the "ugly". A lot of pleasure can be found in recording small objects for their own sake and in making unusual subjects out of those everyday objects we so often taken for granted.

There are potential still-life subjects all around us; it's just that they are often difficult to spot among the clutter of everyday life. It will help to make a cardboard viewfinder (see page 17) and walk around your home with it, looking for anything of interest. The edges of the viewfinder help isolate a small area from its surroundings, and by looking through the small window you can see the design potential of a seemingly random group of objects. You will be amazed at the ready-made subjects all around you.

▲ TIME FOR TEA

This "found" still life had to be drawn quickly, before the meal was eaten and the dishes cleared away. Working quickly forces you to concentrate on the essentials, and results in drawings that are lively and spontaneous.

▶ A GARDENING THEME

Objects with the patina of use and age are often more interesting to the artist than the shiny and the new.

Most drawings use a combination of line and tone to describe the shape and volume of objects. For a beginner, it can be instructive to make two drawings of the same subject, one purely with line and one purely with tone. With line, form and volume are described by linear means; with tone, they are described through the interplay of light and shadow. By exploring the differences between these two approaches, you will find it easier to combine line and tone in an effective way.

Choose an appropriate medium for each drawing: perhaps hard pencil, pen and ink, or felt-tip marker for the line drawing, and charcoal, conté crayon, or graphite stick for the tonal drawing.

When drawing with line, try using it to describe where the edge of one surface meets another. If you just draw a continuous outline, your drawing will look flat and one-dimensional. Broken, irregular lines that vary in weight will suggest the play of light and shadow on an object, as well as accentuating the contours of the bumps and hollows on its surface.

To convey an impression of the volume of an object, let the lines travel across its surface, following its curves, flat surfaces, and indentations. Make use of any patterns or lines on the surface to help define the object's shape. In this instance, the lines of stitching are used to suggest the irregular shapes and undulating surfaces of the shoes.

For the tonal version, don't draw any outlines at all, but use blocks of tone to describe areas of shadow on the shoes. Try to see the subject as a continuously changing pattern of light areas against dark areas and dark against light. Use your chosen medium on its side to make smooth, continuous, evenly graduated areas of tone where surfaces curve and turn.

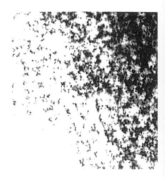

▶ DEFINING SPACE

The cast shadow helps define the edge of the shoe's sole and also serves to separate the two shoes.

◀ DESCRIBING FORM

Carefully modulated tones describe the way light travels across the forms of the shoes. Even the linear aspects—the twisting laces and lines of stitching—are described without any use of line.

▲ FOLLOWING CONTOURS

The lines of stitching on the shoes help to describe their rounded forms.

▶ LOST & FOUND LINES

Lines are not continuous, even where they describe a continuous edge. For example, the broken lines along the side of the shoe suggest the play of light and shadow.

134

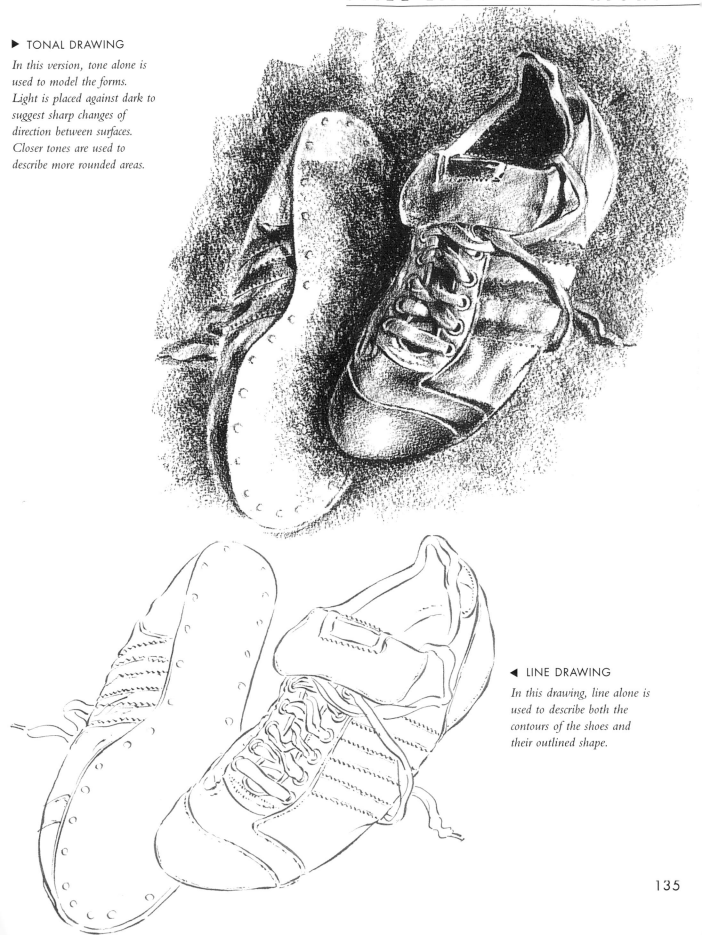

▶ TONAL DRAWING

In this version, tone alone is used to model the forms. Light is placed against dark to suggest sharp changes of direction between surfaces. Closer tones are used to describe more rounded areas.

◀ LINE DRAWING

In this drawing, line alone is used to describe both the contours of the shoes and their outlined shape.

135

FORM & SHAPE

Drawing still-life subjects is an excellent way of practicing your drawing skills. Small-scale objects are more accessible than those encountered in the landscape, and you can study them close up and at leisure. For instance, once you've learned to draw a box in perspective and model its form with light and shade, you can then go on to drawing buildings with renewed confidence.

Spherical objects are among the most difficult shapes to draw accurately, and drawing bottles, cups, pitchers, and plates in a still-life group will give you plenty of practice. A common problem

with these subjects is that of drawing ellipses accurately. To help you understand the perspective of circles and ellipses, hold a clear glass tumbler or bottle and observe how the shapes at the top and the base become wider or flatter as you tip it back and forth. If you look directly onto the top of the glass you will see a circle. But lower your viewpoint slightly and you no longer see a circle but a circle in perspective—an ellipse. The lower your viewpoint, the flatter the ellipse will be.

Since you'll come across ellipses quite often, it is important to learn how to draw them well. The task is easier if you first establish the center line, both vertically and horizontally, as in the diagrams

▶ CIRCLES & ELLIPSES

Perspective affects circles and ellipses in the same way as rectangles. The flatter the angle from which a circle is seen, the more elliptical it becomes.

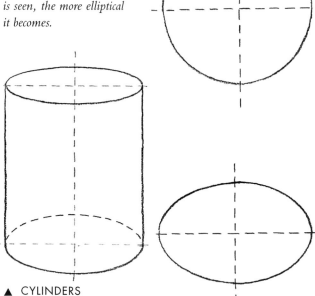

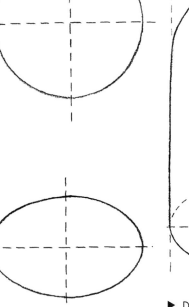

◀ DRAWING ELLIPSES

Ellipses can be drawn freehand on an object such as a bottle by establishing the vertical center line of the bottle, then the horizontal line across the base of the cylinder to give the center of the ellipse. Assess the degree of curve around the bottom and then draw in the ellipse around one quarter of the circumference at a time, making sure the fullest part of the ellipse falls in the center at front and back.

▲ CYLINDERS

When a standing cylindrical object is viewed from slightly above, the ellipse that is closer is seen from a flatter angle, and is therefore narrower from front to back than the ellipse at the end that is further away.

▶ DRAWING THROUGH

To create a convincing three-dimensional effect, act as though your subject is transparent and capture the underlying structure as well as the outer shape. In this way you "feel" the sense of weight and volume, and your drawing will be more accurate.

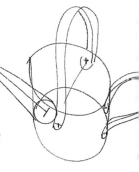

◄ MODELING A CUBE

The three visible sides of this cube are defined by clearly distinguished light, mid and dark tones of the same color. The tone has been built up gradually by putting a light wash over all three sides, a mid-tone over two sides, and a dark tone over one side.

► MODELING SPHERES, CONES & CYLINDERS

Spheres, cones, and cylinders have gradually curving surfaces, and are modeled through smooth gradations in tone. The progression from light to dark creates the impression of a solid, rounded object. The reflected light on the side opposite the highlight is essential for conveying a fully three-dimensional effect.

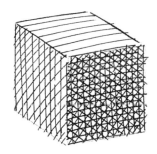

◄ LINEAR METHODS

Here shading is built up with hatched and crosshatched lines. The denser the lines, the darker the tone appears.

► CROSSHATCHING

Try using crosshatching to describe gently curving forms by building up the tone from light to dark as the surface turns away from the light. Start by hatching in one direction over the whole form, breaking it where the highlight falls. Lay another layer at a different angle over all but the lightest area, another over the darker areas and so on, until you have captured the depth of tone of the darkest shadows.

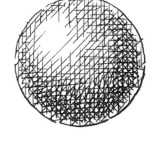

on the opposite page. Don't press hard with your pencil and try to draw the ellipse in a single line, but hold the pencil lightly and "feel out" the form as you draw. Keep your wrist and pencil fixed. Let your elbow provide the sideways movement, and move your arm back and forth at the shoulder. Use light, feathery strokes and go over the lines again if necessary until you are satisfied that the shape is correct. Remember that an ellipse is curved all the way round—avoid the common mistake of making the ends pointed, like a football.

Once you are confident about drawing shapes and outlines accurately, you can move on to describing

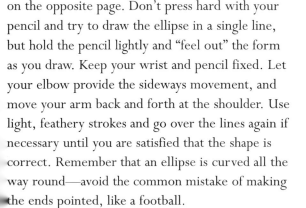

◄ ▲ CONTOUR DRAWING

Lines that travel across the surface of an object, following the contours, can convey its shape and volume.

4B PENCIL

PASTEL

COLORED PENCILS

4B CHISEL-END PENCIL

CHALKS IN WARM GRAYS

BROAD-TIPPED
CALLIGRAPHY PEN

6B GRAPHITE STICK

MEDIA & TECHNIQUES

Take a single object and experiment with a range of different media and techniques, both broad and linear, for describing its three-dimensional form.

7B PENCIL

BALLPOIN PEN

form and volume. How do you go about describing solid, three-dimensional forms on a flat piece of paper? The answer lies in using tone—degrees of light and dark—to show the way light strikes the various planes and surfaces of objects, creating shadows and highlights. By using a full range of tones from light to dark, you can show which parts of an object are closest to the source of light and which are farther away and thus create the illusion of solid, three-dimensional reality. When it comes to drawing seemingly complex subjects—flowers, fruits, figures, animals, trees, clouds—it helps to visualize them first as simple geometric shapes. All the objects around us are combinations of the curves and planes found in the simplest geometric shapes: the sphere, the cone, the cylinder, and the cube. A bottle is basically a cylinder, fruits are mostly spherical or near-spherical, a building is basically a cube, and so on. Once you understand how to model these simple forms with light and shade, you will find it much easier to apply the same principles to less easily defined forms.

The cube is the simplest form to render as a solid object using light and shade, since its flat faces and straight edges can be drawn easily and the planes show distinct changes of tone. Rounded forms are slightly more difficult because the tonal gradations are much more subtle. At the point closest to the light source you have the highlight. From here, there is a gradual transition from halftone to shadow as the object turns away from the light, which describes the smooth curve of the surface. Light striking the surface on which the object rests, or a nearby surface, bounces back into the shadow side, creating a thin sliver of lighter tone at the extreme edge of the shadow area. This is known as reflected light, and is a valuable when drawing rounded form.

▼ LINE & WASH

Use linear marks to describe structure, texture, and details, overlaid with washes to suggest light and shade and give solidity to the forms. Leave the highlights as white paper. Line and wash is a very expressive technique; try it with pen and ink or pencil and watercolor.

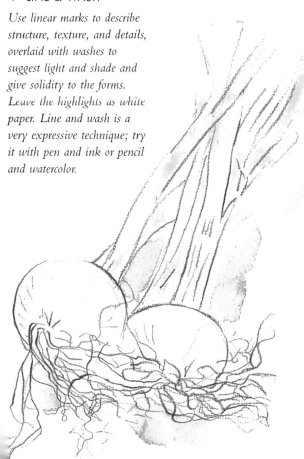

▲ SUBTLE SHADING

In this carefully built up drawing, the artist conveys the subtle variations in light and shade. A soft graphite stick is excellent for modeling forms because it gives a full range of tones, from a soft whisper of gray to the deepest black.

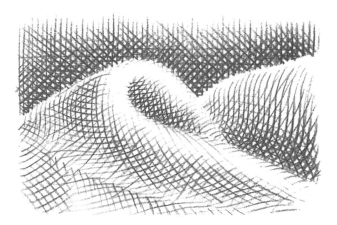

▲ DIRECTIONAL LINES

It is always an interesting exercise to describe rounded forms using a linear technique. Here, the direction of the hatching lines follows the curving lines of the cloth, and the lines are always made at an angle to the surface being described, not parallel with the edges.

EXPLORING TEXTURES

Most still-life groups contain a variety of objects, each with its own particular texture: the smooth surface of porcelain, the bright sheen of metal, the rough graininess of wood, the soft folds of fabric, and so on. If you want your pictures to look convincing, it is important to render such textures accurately. The idea is not to attempt a photographic copy of an object, but to combine strokes and tones so that they suggest the quality of its surface and, at the same time, give your drawing a lively, active surface interest of its own.

You can create an illusion of texture not only by using different marks and strokes, but also by suggesting the ways in which different surfaces reflect light. For example, convey the hard, smooth, polished surface of metal by accentuating tonal contrasts and by creating fairly sharp divisions between one patch of tone and another, keeping your shading as smooth and even as possible. In contrast, wood doesn't reflect much light, so avoid strong contrasts of light and shade by subtly blending your tones. Suggest the rough, grainy texture of the wood by streaking in darker lines of varying length and thickness.

The nature of the paper surface can also enhance textural effects. Smooth textures, such as those of metal and glass, fruits, and soft cloth are continuous, so it makes sense to choose a smooth cartridge paper and build up delicate shading with a hard pencil.

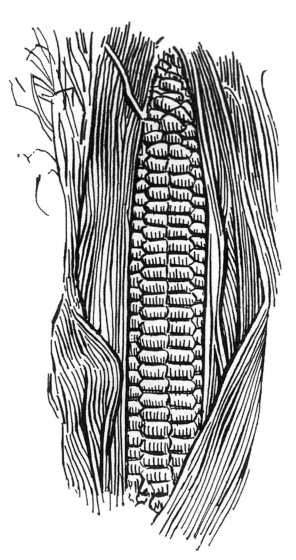

◀ LINE & WASH

Combining line and tone in one drawing is an excellent way to describe structure, texture, and details in a lively way. Here, ink lines define the glass and grapes, and the washes describe the wine in the glass, with reflected colors on the rim and base. The paper has been left white in places for the highlights.

▲ PEN & INK

A very detailed study of an ear of corn has been drawn here with a steel-nibbed pen on smooth paper. The artist has effectively captured the contrast between the fibrous, papery texture of the outer husk and the hard, knobbly texture of the corn kernels inside.

▶ CHARCOAL & PASTEL

You can mix different media in one drawing to create a particular texture or quality. Here, for example, charcoal and pastel merge to produce an impression of form as well as the smooth, hard texture of the apple. Charcoal and pastel are both soft, easily blended media that combine well with each other.

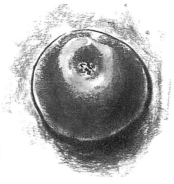

▼ WAX RESIST

The pitted texture of lemons is captured perfectly using the technique of wax resist. Apply a wash of yellow watercolor to rough-textured watercolor paper and allow to dry. Then "draw" the lemons with a wax candle, skimming it lightly over the paper. Apply a green watercolor wash on top; the wax resists the watercolor, magically revealing the shapes and textures of the lemons.

▼ PASTEL & INK

The smooth flow of ink and the grainy marks of pastel are another winning combination. These strawberries were painted with colored ink; when the ink dried, the tiny seeds on their surface were picked out with touches of hard pastel.

Rough-textured papers are uneven and broken, and soft pencils, chalks, and charcoal can be dragged across the paper on their sides to create a broken effect that successfully describes the pitted skin of oranges and lemons, or the roughness of a piece of driftwood.

When planning a still-life group, try to avoid compositions in which all the elements have the same kind of texture. If you place rough and smooth surfaces side by side—soft fruits in a wicker basket, for example—they will look more realistic because of the contrast (the rough enhances the smooth and vice versa), and your finished drawing will be much more interesting to look at.

When planning a still-life study, decide which approach you want to take—realistic, loose and expressive, or abstract—and which aspects you want to emphasize—the surface qualities and textures, the structure, or the shapes and patterns found within the subject. Then choose the materials and techniques that you think will best bring these out. Smooth, reflective surfaces can be modeled with carefully graduated tones using pencil or charcoal. Or you can use line to make a carefully observed drawing of the structure of the object. For an abstract approach, concentrate on the shapes of the different parts of the group, moving in close and framing the composition so that the shapes are cropped off by the edges of the paper.

This project looks at the ways in which a simple household object—a coffee press—can provide material for an imaginative, abstract composition. Three separate aspects of the subject are explored and then combined in a semiabstract composition. Pencil is used for a realistic rendition in the left-hand press, while brush and ink are used for a loose, expressive interpretation of the right-hand press. Finally, the shapes and patterns within the subject, such as the holes in the plunger and the wire mesh of the filter, are used to develop an abstract background worked in colored pencils.

◄ DETAIL

Fine details are meticulously described through smooth blending and tonal contrasts.

▶ TONAL WASHES

Loose tonal washes serve to create a sense of volume and solidity as well as convey the shiny surface of metal.

▲ ABSTRACTS

The internal workings are blown up and rearranged into an abstract pattern that forms an unusual background.

▲ SHAPES & PATTERNS

A pencil drawing with tonal blending and attention to detail produces a photorealistic effect, while a loose drawing with brush and ink captures the volume and character of the coffee press. With each individual part rearranged, it is possible to see the subject as a series of shapes and patterns that can be developed with different colors and marks.

◀ REFLECTIONS

The reflections in the lid are captured with controlled pencil shading.

FLOWERS & PLANTS

Flowers and plants are the most popular ingredients of still-life studies. Their wonderful shapes, colors, and textures are always inspiring, no matter whether you draw a single daffodil in a coffee jar or a lavish display of roses in a crystal vase.

To draw flowers convincingly, you need to understand their structure. You can easily fill a sketchbook with detailed studies of individual flowers, leaves, stems, buds, and seedheads in close-up, and it will give you invaluable insight into botanical form and structure. Be aware of the subtle nuances. Observe how the leaf stalks join the main stem of the plant, and how the petals are arranged. Note how the leaves are arranged along the stem: in some plants they are arranged in pairs, in others they are arranged alternately. Texture is important,

too: some leaves are smooth, others are hairy; some thin and fragile, others tough and leathery.

Because flowers are so intricate and complex, the temptation is to describe every leaf and petal in minute detail. This is fine when you are making a botanical study, but it is inappropriate for a still-life drawing, where your aim is to express qualities such as softness, delicacy and transience. With practice you will soon learn how to capture, with a few expressive strokes, a flower's essential characteristics.

Flowers in a still-life drawing should be arranged

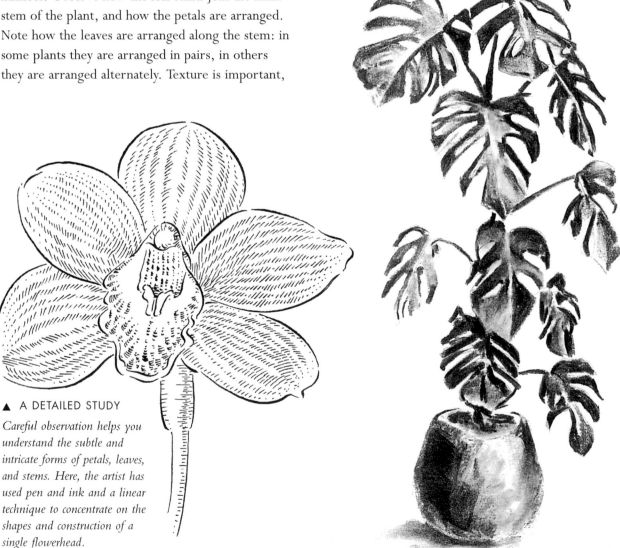

▲ A DETAILED STUDY
Careful observation helps you understand the subtle and intricate forms of petals, leaves, and stems. Here, the artist has used pen and ink and a linear technique to concentrate on the shapes and construction of a single flowerhead.

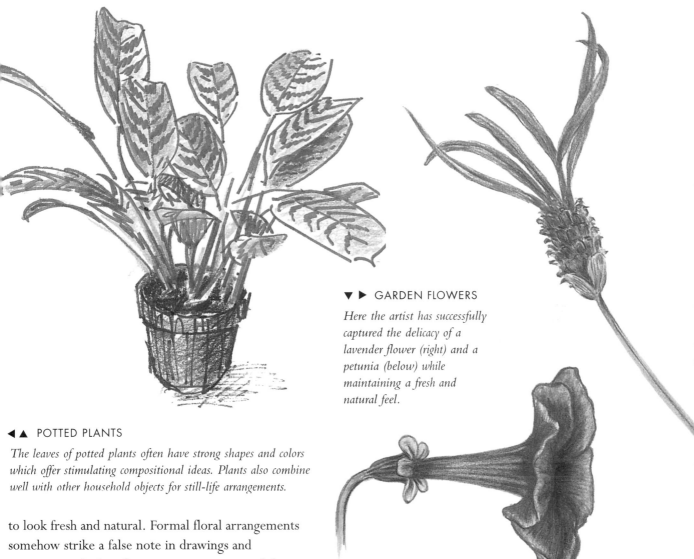

▼ ▶ GARDEN FLOWERS

Here the artist has successfully captured the delicacy of a lavender flower (right) and a petunia (below) while maintaining a fresh and natural feel.

◀▲ POTTED PLANTS

The leaves of potted plants often have strong shapes and colors which offer stimulating compositional ideas. Plants also combine well with other household objects for still-life arrangements.

to look fresh and natural. Formal floral arrangements somehow strike a false note in drawings and paintings, and when flowers are over-arranged they lose the delicate, living quality that is their greatest charm. Don't cram too many flowers into the vase; choose just a few blooms and let them fall naturally, allowing some to overlap others and placing them at different heights, with some of the heads turned away from you, as they would appear when growing in a garden.

If you are working in a color medium such as pastel, plan the color scheme of your setup carefully. As a rule of thumb, it is best to choose one predominant color for the flowers and echo this in the background, perhaps adding just a touch of contrasting color here and there.

When you draw a vase of flowers, try to convey

the impression that some of the blooms are farther back than others. This is achieved by bringing the closer flowers into sharp focus while playing down those farther back in the group; if every flower is given equal emphasis, the feeling of three-dimensional form is lost and the flowers appear hard and brittle. Pick out one or two flowers near the front and emphasize these with crisp, "found" edges. Make the flowers farther back less well-defined by using soft, "lost" edges. This "lost and found" quality of line essentially gives a sense of the flowers being living, growing things and adds a touch of poetry to your drawings.

The colors of flowers and plants are subtly varied, and change according to the quality of the prevailing light. A single leaf, for example, is never the same green all over; it shifts from a cool, dark green on the shadowed parts to a warm, light green in the light parts. When observing your subject, try to analyze its colors in terms of tone and emperature. Don't look at a color in isolation but compare it with the colors around it. Ask yourself questions: is that particular leaf light or dark compared with the leaves around it? Does that pink rose tend towards a warm orange or a cool violet? Look, too, for places where reflected colors are being picked up either from another part of the subject or from the surroundings. By observing and recording these subtle modulations of color, your drawings of flowers and plants will appear more realistically and lifelike.

Rather than filling in areas of solid color, do as the Impressionists did and build up an area with separate strokes of color. For example, use strokes of blue and yellow to make green, or blue and red to make purple. This is called optical mixing, because all the colors are visible and mix in the viewer's eye. Because the colors are separate, they resonate on the eye and so appear more vibrant.

Colored pencils have been chosen for this project because they combine ease of use and direct application of color with the potential to create a wide range of colors and tones through hatching and crosshatching. Have a good selection of the colors present in your subject, and work on a smooth or slightly textured paper to get the very best results.

Choose a plant with vibrant or unusual colors and strong, clearly defined shapes within the flowers and leaves, and set it in front of a simple background. Begin by making an outline drawing in pencil to establish the main shapes. Then block in the main areas of color, leaving highlights as white paper for the time being. Next, work back into the shapes to establish the volumes, using darker tones of the same colors. The final stage is to introduce reflected colors from the surroundings in the areas where you

▲ BUILDING UP

Colors can be mixed by adding one on top of the other. Work lightly so that the underlying color shows through the top layer.

▶ HATCHING

Loose hatching using the points of colored pencils creates a more lively effect than solid shading.

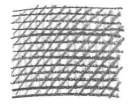

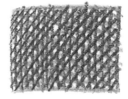

◀ CROSSHATCHING

Vibrant color effects are achieved by crosshatching with different colors. Above left, red, yellow, and blue have been crosshatched in a horizontal, vertical, and diagonal direction. Below left, four contrasting hues create a shimmering web of color.

see them. Develop the background at the same rate as the main subject so that you can judge one against the other.

To get your colors to mix optically on the paper, develop the drawing by building up a web of finely hatched lines using the points of the pencils, rather than making areas of continuous shading. In this project, the hatching varies in direction all over the drawing, which allows the color to work to its full effect in modeling the volumes of the plant. Keep the hatching fairly loose, and try to treat the subject as a pattern of different-colored shapes with light, dark and reflected-color modulations worked into them.

▲ CREATING THE SHAPE

The main shapes of the cactus are drawn in with a soft gray pencil that will disappear under the colored drawing.

◄ COLOR HATCHING

The general contours in each area are established, and the colors are kept almost flat. The flower is hatched in with a red pencil, leaving the lightest areas as white paper, and the colors in the centre are just hinted at. The leaves are hatched in with green, with slight indications of shadow, and the background is put in with loosely hatched strokes of indigo blue.

▼ BUILDING UP COLOR

Form and volume is developed by building up strokes, strengthening the existing colors. Blue is added into the greens on the leaf nodules in the shadow areas to make them appear rounded. The background is worked up at the same rate as the plant so that the two are integrated.

▲ REFLECTED COLOR

Reflected colors are introduced into the plant and the background, for instance on the leaves facing the flower, which have touches of red worked into them. The colors are intensified in the center of the flower to define it.

◀ WARM COLOR

Reflected colors from the plant are worked into the background to give it depth and intensity, and warm colors are added into the spikes and some of the leaves.

▶ LIGHT & DARK

A richly woven web of multidirectional hatching across the whole drawing produces an image of great depth and luminosity, in which light and dark and warm and cool colors model the intricate forms of the plant.

◀ DETAIL

Red is worked into the green of the leaves where they are reflecting color from the flower above.

▼ CREATING DEPTH

Large areas of the paper are left white in the flower. Depth is suggested at the centre through light and dark tones.

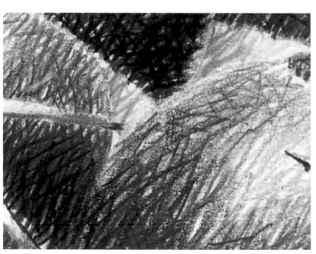

▲ WARM & COOL

The nodules are suggested with cool, dark blue-greens in the shadow areas, and pale, warm greens in the light areas.

INTERIORS

If you are looking for exciting subjects to draw, you don't have to look further than your own home. Domestic interiors offer marvelous opportunities for creating interesting and unusual arrangements of light, color, and perspective.

As with still lifes, domestic interiors offer the advantage of allowing you to control the compositional arrangement of the subject, as well as the lighting. The following are just some ideas worth considering: open doors and windows offering tantalizing glimpses of scenes beyond the room; shafts of light that highlight certain objects; interesting angles and intersections formed by furniture, carpets, pictures and so on.

Remember the laws of perspective and apply them to all sets of parallel lines. There is no natural horizon line in a room as there is in a landscape, so use the old trick of holding a pencil, horizontally, in front of your eyes; its position will coincide with the horizon line. Lightly draw the horizon line on

◄ A ROOM WITH A VIEW

An interior scene takes on a whole new dimension when you include the additional space that can be seen through a window or an open doorway. The distant view outside increases the feeling of depth and space and serves to draw the viewer deeper into the picture.

◀ CAFÉ SOCIETY

Interiors of public buildings are fascinating because they combine elements of still life and figure painting. Take your sketchbook with you when you go out. Good subjects include train stations, cafés, and restaurant, theaters, galleries and museums, churches and cathedrals, to name just a few.

▶ HOME SWEET HOME

The light in the enclosed environment of a room often has a soft, luminous quality, which is effectively captured in this conté drawing. Try drawing the same room at different times of the day and note how the lights and shadows subtly change as the day progresses.

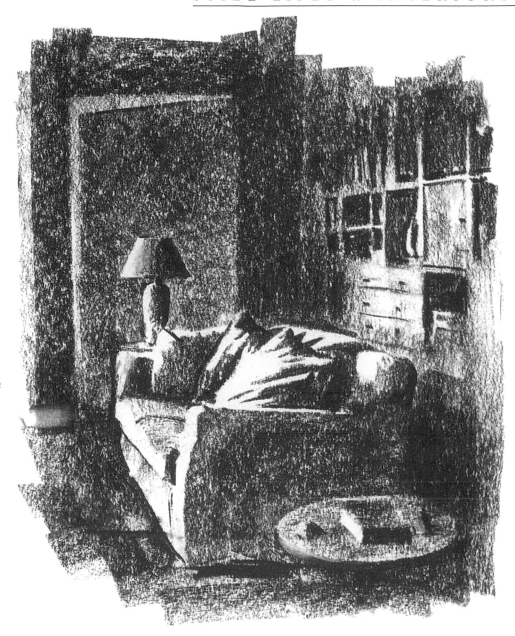

your paper, then draw the vertical and horizontal lines of walls, doors, and windows facing you. Draw the receding lines of the side walls; if continued, they should meet at the vanishing point on the horizon line (see page 16 for more information on linear perspective).

By including the view through a door or window in your picture you create an intriguing double image—a frame within a frame. There is often a strong contrast between interior and exterior because bright light outside intensifies the darkness within. Thus, to convey a sense of strong light outside, you need to deepen the tones of the interior. Plan the tonal organization of the drawing before you begin. The strongest contrast of light and dark tone will attract the eye, so decide where you want the center of interest to fall and place the lightest light against the darkest dark there. With this type of subject, this contrast will occur where light from the window meets the interior. Tones in the rest of the drawing should fall between these two extremes.

Views through windows, which are almost like pictures within pictures, offer excellent subjects and have great potential for exploring aspects of composition and space—inside and out.

For this project, take a few objects that are varied in size and tone and have interesting shapes and place them on a table in front of a window. The tabletop in this project drawing is highly reflective, which introduces reflections as well as shadows into the composition. Arrange the objects in an interesting way and position one or two objects so that you see them framed against the window.

As you draw your setup, concentrate on assessing the correct tones. Remember to judge the individual tones in your subject against others, both nearby and in other parts of the scene. The aim is to create an impression of bright light shining in from outside, creating strong contrasts between light and dark in the area just inside the window. To make the view seen through the window appear much

farther away than the objects inside the room, make the tones much lighter and less contrasting in the distance and reduce the level of detail and texture.

Use charcoal and a lightly textured paper with enough "tooth" to hold the charcoal without smudging too easily. Use increased pressure and layering to develop depth of tone in the shadow

▶ PLANNING THE COMPOSITION

A compositional sketch is done in three tones in order to plan where the strongest contrasts occur. The center of interest is the tabletop with the objects reflected in it, so the main light/dark contrasts occur here.

▲ BUILDING UP THE DRAWING

The position of the main objects in the composition is established with a series of light pencil lines.

▲ MID- & LIGHT TONES

Having established light to dark tonal ranges, mid- and lighter tones are introduced. The area through the window is lighter than the interior so that it recedes into the distance.

▲ DARK TONES

The darkest areas, which occur within the room, are simply blocked in as general solid shapes.

areas. If it is difficult to build up enough layers of charcoal, fix the drawing with spray fixative (see page 11) at an intermediate stage to keep what you have done in place while you continue to work. You can also use a kneaded eraser as a drawing tool along with the charcoal. Use it to take out highlights in areas that have been overworked, as well as to blend tones and create marks and texture by working into areas of charcoal.

▲ BLENDING

Areas of tone have been blended to give a softer, less textural effect. This is particularly obvious in the objects on the table, the chair to the left, and the carpet.

▲ SILHOUETTES

The lamp silhouetted against the view outside helps create a sense of distance.

▼ LINKED TOGETHER

No shape on the table, positive or negative, is seen in isolation. They overlap each other, or are linked by shadows and reflections.

▲ UNIFYING FACTOR

The plant serves to knit together the foreground and the background.

▶ CONTRAST

The background is sketched in light tones that contrast not only with the interior, but also with the tree outside the window, creating an impression of deep space between the plane of the window and the far distance.

▲ TONE & REFLECTION

The reflection of the tree outside the window has been added on the table. Strong contrasts within the room are used to suggest strong light outside, and the whole image is built through the juxtaposition of blocks of tone.

AERIAL PERSPECTIVE

The way in which the atmosphere reduces the strength of the tones and colors that we see as they recede into the distance. This phenomenon is used in drawings to describe receding space by making the tones progressively lighter as the subject recedes towards the horizon.

BRIGHTNESS

This term is usually used in reference to color. It refers to a color's saturation, or strength, and is measured from full strength to very muted. It shouldn't be confused with tone, which refers to a color's lightness or darkness.

COMPLEMENTARY COLOR

Colors that are opposite each other on the color wheel are referred to as complementary. The complementary pairs are red and green, blue and orange, and violet and yellow. Each pair contains all three primary colors.

COMPOSITION

The process of arranging the different elements in the picture into a design that leads or draws the eye to the main area of interest.

CONTRAST

The placing of two opposites next to each other: light next to dark, a small shape next to a large one, a bright color next to a dull one, a rough texture next to a smooth one. Contrast of any sort creates a focus of interest within the picture that draws the viewer's eye.

CROSSHATCHING

Lines are drawn parallel to each other across an area of the drawing, and another set of lines is drawn over the top at an angle to the first ones. Layers can be built up in this way until the area has become as dark or dense as you want it to be.

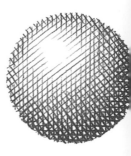

FORM

The three-dimensional nature of objects. The form of an object is revealed by light falling across it, illuminating some surfaces while others remain in shadow.

HARMONY

Similar tones, colors, shapes, textures, and so on—the opposite of contrast. Harmonious areas do not draw attention in the way that contrasts do, and balanced compositions contain both harmony and contrast.

HUE

The color of a particular paint or chalk—red, yellow, green, and so on.

KEY

The tonal mood of a picture. High-key pictures are pitched at the lighter end of the tonal scale, while low-key pictures are pitched at the darker end. In both, the range of tones is condensed to a few, although touches of the other may be included for contrast.

LINEAR PERSPECTIVE

A method of depicting three-dimensional objects on a two-dimensional surface. It is based on the fact that parallel lines running away from the viewer appear to converge toward the horizon. As a result, objects or parts of objects that are farther away from the viewer look smaller than those that are close. It can also be used to draw objects in the correct scale.

MONOCHROME

Literally, one color. It is most commonly used to describe a black-and-white image, but it includes any image done in a single color, including a drawing done in different tones of the same color.

PLANE

A flat surface. Objects are made up of many planes, all facing different directions. Changes in plane can be abrupt, such as two sides of a cube, or curved and gradual, such as a sphere. Changes of plane in an object, either abrupt or gradual, are perceived through changes in tone.

PRIMARY COLORS

The three primary colors are red, yellow, and blue. They are called primary colors because they are the only colors that cannot be made by mixing together other colors in the palette.

SCUMBLING

A layer of thin or semi-transparent color—pastels or paint—is applied over another color so that the color underneath shows through.

SECONDARY COLORS

The colors made by mixing two primary colors: green, mixed from blue and yellow; violet, mixed from blue and red; and orange, mixed from red and yellow.

TERTIARY COLORS

The colors that are made by mixing two adjacent primary and secondary colors.

TONE

The lightness or darkness of an object or area, regardless of its color. In relation to objects, it also refers to the amount of light being reflected by a surface.

TOOTH

A paper with a rough or textured surface is described as having "tooth".

WASH

An area of transparent paint, such as watercolor or thin acrylic, laid across the paper with a paintbrush. Washes can be used to prepare paper for drawing on, or applied as part of the drawing itself. Washes can be layered one over another.

Index compiled by Lydia Darbyshire